Spreading My Wings

Spreading My Wings

Joel Whitwell

Copyright © 2024 Joel Whitwell

All rights reserved. No part of this book may be reproduced or transmitted in any form or by any means, electronic or mechanical, including photocopying, recording, or by any information storage and retrieval system without the written permission of the author, except where permitted by law.

This book is a collection of memories. The personal stories and memories by individuals recorded here are their version of events and have been both provided and reproduced in good faith with no disrespect or defamation intended. Every effort has been made to ensure the researched information is correct. No liability for incorrect information or factual errors will be accepted by the author.

Publishing Details
Spreading My Wings

 A catalogue record for this book is available from the National Library of Australia

ISBN 9780645036428 (paperback)
ISBN 9780645036435 (ebook)

This second book is again dedicated to my family who have never wavered in their support of me, and to the memory of Cara Hales who always saw the beauty in life such as a field of sunflowers in the Spring. Shine on, you beautiful diamond.

Cara

Table of Contents

Introduction ············ ix
Preface ············ xi

One	The Beginning of a New Chapter	1
Two	Time to Fly	4
Three	Toowoomba Lads	8
Four	Aberystwyth, the Hidden Gem	11
Five	London Bound	14
Six	Another Hard Goodbye	16
Seven	Time to Heal and Grow	18
Eight	White Ninja	20
Nine	An English Rose	23
Ten	Amsterdam, Here I Come!	26
Eleven	Shooting Stars and Extraterrestrials	28
Twelve	High on Life and Friendships	31
Thirteen	Home Time	35
Fourteen	The Snowball Effect	36
Fifteen	Tragedy Strikes	39
Sixteen	Life Begins at 40	41
Seventeen	Footy Fever	45
Eighteen	Scaling Mount Franklin	50
Nineteen	Cheers to PJ	85
Twenty	Oh Canada!	89
Twenty-One	Time to Catch Up	91

Twenty-Two	Vivid Sydney	95
Twenty-Three	Heading Back to The Lads	97
Twenty-Four	Old Habits Do Die Hard	101
Twenty-Five	Cruising Along the Dusty Roads in the Volvo	104
Twenty-Six	Free as a Bird	108
Twenty-Seven	All the Vets and a Meat Inspector	112
Twenty-Eight	Going Down the Rabbit Hole	116
Twenty-Nine	Taking Control of My Own Destiny	120
Thirty	The Virus Strikes	123
Thirty-One	Magnum PI	131
Thirty-Two	Not in Kansas Anymore	133
Thirty-Three	That Wonderful Afternoon at a Park in Dubbo	136
Thirty-Four	Phoenix Rising from the Ashes	139
Thirty-Five	Like a Man in Motion	144
Thirty-Six	The Power of a Friendship Bracelet	152
Thirty-Seven	The Stars Align	156
Thirty-Eight	The World is Your Oyster	163
	Editor's Note	167

Introduction

—Katie Edwards

Joel..
I don't exactly remember the first time I ever met Joel though I do remember him always being a prominent male figure in my life for many years.

We grew up together in a small town called Harvey, south of Perth. You knew everyone and everyone knew you.

Joel was a few years older than me, but I always remember him being so nice and having so many great friendships. Not too long after I was lucky enough to be included in that friendship. We played mixed netball together, we socialized together and thankfully to social media we remained in contact while our lives went on different paths.

I have always watched Joel's travelling adventures and admired him so much for just taking life and making it happen. So many people with a poor me attitude yet my dear friend Joel with zero cares in the world just out there doing things and going places I will most likely only ever dream of.

Little did I know that while he was on one of his adventures, he wasn't dealing with life as well as I thought, and I just couldn't bear the thought of the world losing someone so important and as kind as him.

I too was in my element, I had just had my second baby, and I was absolutely in love with my children and where my life was headed. Though I often found at night while alone and sleep deprived I wasn't coping as well as I had liked. So, randomly, I reached out to Joel one day and funnily enough we had a great chat over socials, and we found some happiness to awaken in both our lives.

We often chat about this and how you should never judge or compare your life with others because deep down everyone has their own little life hurdles to get through. No-one is ever completely ecstatic with their life choices at all given times.

What I see Joel's life as, I admire, and what he sees mine as, he admires. We are both living our lives the way our journey is supposed to, taking every opportunity given to us. But mostly I feel that this friendship is what will forever keep each other grounded. With Joel in my life showing me what he can do, what he will do and what he does do, gives me hope that one day, I too might be brave enough to do some of these things.

As long as Joel continues to reach out when he has his bad days, I will always be there for him.

We don't need to see each other every day, though I know no matter where he is, near or far, I can send him a message and he will do anything to make it all better. He is the definition of a true friend. I hope everyone has the chance to meet him at some point. If you spot him, do yourself a favour and go say hi. Your life will be that little bit better from that point.

Preface

I grew up in a small town and ended up choosing my own path
And when I look back over all the good times I have enjoyed, I always sit back and have a laugh.

For there are worse things you can do in life than reaching for the sky
And when I remember all the memories, it always seems to bring a tear to my eye.

For whenever I have gone through the darkness, I never lost sight of the light.
And when it is time to dream again, I spread my wings and take flight.

One

The Beginning of a New Chapter

From what has happened in my life these last few years from where I was in early 2018 when I concluded my first book, I felt it was only natural to start writing another one! I was in a pretty good place with a recent run of positive and big events happening in my life. First it was the TED talk, followed by the "wonder" fundraiser with Cassie, then delivering the donation to Princess Margaret Hospital for Children. It felt wonderful to get the chance to give back to the hospital that did so much for me in my formative years. You could say I was "on a roll" as the snowball effect was certainly gathering momentum.

In early 2018 I was also living with my brother Frog and his partner Michayla in Galway Green and they had recently had a baby girl who they named Jaycee Jean. I was an uncle again! Living with a toddler in the house wasn't anything I thought it would be. It was great and pretty cool. Frog did spare me some of the messier duties like changing her nappies, I was lucky in that regard. I also got to hold her, and I loved taking photographs with her in my arms. There was a park just down the road where we would often take Jaycee for a walk. Life was bliss. At this time, I was still working as a government meat inspector. I would often travel around with my job which suited me just fine. My old friend Calvin Rodgers lived not too far away in Australind, so one Friday night I caught a taxi around to his place where we indulged in another drinking session. I guess some things never change.

I was keeping in touch with friends I had made overseas. Even though I had heard of a "video call", Facetime and Zoom, back then, my mode of contact with friends overseas was always via a Facebook message. Lauren was a lady from New Zealand I met on my Contiki tour through the USA with Luke back in 2014. So one night I decided to send her a message and almost straight away my phone started ringing. It was Lauren calling me on Facetime. That was unexpected, so you can imagine my surprise. I started freaking out. I didn't know what to do. I was dead sober. Should I answer? Or let it ring out? I could feel my heart pounding. This wasn't meant to happen. Why didn't she just reply with a Facebook message like she usually does? That was the norm. By this stage my anxiety and paranoia had really started to kick in. What should I do? I had to think fast as it was about to ring out.

As has often been the case in my life, I decided to take a chance and answer. As soon as I did, I saw Lauren came up on the screen. It looked like she was sitting in the back seat of a car. "Oh hey," she casually said when she saw me. This seemed like a normal thing for her, which it probably was for everyone besides me.

"Hi," I replied. She then told me that she had been at a party where she had drunk a little too much, got sick and decided to sleep it off in a friend's car when my message came through. Hence the call back. "Okay," I thought. We got chatting and I started to relax.

I was enjoying this new and exciting mode of contact that Lauren had just introduced me to and we ended up chatting for a while, mainly about the memories we made on the Contiki tour and what we had done in our lives since then. Lauren was a bit drunk while I was sober, so this was also new territory for me, but we managed to pull it off and it was an enjoyable conversation.

After I hung up, I told myself I would never get that worked up and paranoid over a video call again. Since then, I have done a few more video calls and Zooms (another way of staying in contact with people) and a couple of live streams sharing my story, so thank you once again Lauren for what you were able to start that night by for introducing me to this new world!

Two

Time to Fly

In the meantime, I was starting to get itchy feet. I longed for travel and couldn't wait to get back out there again. My work always went quiet around July, so I decided to plan my next trip for that time. I always enjoy the planning as that is when the excitement starts to build. I was keeping in touch with my friend Emily from the UK who I had met in Spain the year before, and of course Shaun Attwood was also there, so I was most definitely heading back to the UK. I also settled on a Top Deck tour through Ireland and Wales as my new destination. And, what the hell, I decided to head back to Amsterdam for "old times sake". I have always had a good relationship with that city!

What another great adventure this was already shaping up to be. I couldn't wait to get back out there. By this stage I had discovered that my main passions in life were travelling and writing. As mentioned in my first book, I was now fully aware of, and had finally taken the steps, to get on top of my binge drinking. Step by step I was winning, but then it dawned on me where I was about to travel. Ireland. It seemed to have a bigger reputation when it came to drinking than anywhere else in the world! Their culture was renowned for it. Oh well, sometimes you need to set the bar high in life and what better place to see where exactly I was at with my binge drinking than Ireland! Bring it on, I say!

Not long before my departure, I was explaining to Mum that I was heading to Belfast where the *Titanic* was built. Her reply was "Wow. Are you going to see the *Titanic*?" Haha. I had a big laugh at that one! Got to love Mum.

Finally, I boarded the plane for the big adventure. By this point I really had come into my own as a solo traveller and embraced it. My trip to Scandinavia and Iceland a few years earlier had been my litmus test for solo travel, and I had grown since then. I was still hoping to catch up with Shaun, Richard and Emily. This time I had to transit in Doha and Heathrow. Ahh, so many wonderful memories in that airport as they all came flooding back. I finally landed in Belfast late in the day and as I caught a taxi to my hotel the driver pointed out some of the major attractions in the city including the docks where they built the *Titanic* off in the distance. I was impressed. When he dropped me at my hotel, he motioned towards the pub next door and told me that for my best interests I shouldn't go in there as it was known to be violent and inhabited by shadowy characters. That only meant one thing to this extreme traveller – I was going into that pub at some point.

The *Titanic* is a big part of Belfast's history, so I spent my first day checking out the museum and dock's where it was built. Another part of Belfast's recent history was "The Troubles" otherwise known as the "Northern Ireland Conflicts". It was between the Unionists and the Republicans and lasted about 30 years before an agreement was made between the parties in 1998. So, this city had mostly found peace in the 20 years preceding my visit. I also felt that vibe. After all they had been through, I found the locals very friendly and welcoming. I lapped it up and was in my element. I went on a bus tour which took us past the house where the famous soccer player George Best grew up. Belfast wasn't a big city, but it was leaving a good impression on me. I also had to try a good ol' Irish Guinness while I was there. It had a different taste to the Guinness back home. It was more of an acquired taste

A few days into the trip I was walking past a pub around midday when I decided to pop in for a bit of lunch and a quiet beer. I couldn't believe it. It was Tuesday which constituted a working day, and the place was packed! It was filled with patrons. I wondered if everyone had knocked off work early, but then the pub started going quiet as patrons stumbled out the door, so I figured they were on their lunch break. "How good is the Irish culture?" I thought as I sipped on my beer. Spending your lunch break socialising at the pub would certainly ease a lot of the stress encountered in your workday! The Irish were onto something, I thought.

After a while of sitting there on my own a couple of blokes sitting at a table across the room motioned for me to join them, which I happily did. I found them to both be great blokes and interesting characters as I found out a bit about their lives. One was a stand-up comedian who sounded like he was well-known around Belfast as people kept coming up to chat with him. He certainly was funny and outgoing. I felt blessed in that moment for always being able to meet interesting people on my travels. It was an enjoyable afternoon, especially when the topic of the *Titanic* came up as the pair seemed pleased by that part of their history, which I found fascinating as it was deemed the "unsinkable ship" which had in fact sunk in April 1912 There was plenty of backslapping and good cheer. I was in my element.

After a few hours things were starting to get a bit rowdy, and as I didn't want to go back to my old habit of drinking too much, I excused myself and walked back to my hotel. It was evening when I arrived back, and I was feeling a bit tipsy and decided to go somewhere for dinner. I looked over at the pub next door and remembered what the taxi driver had told me when he dropped me off. I was going in, so I armed myself with my phone, wallet and room key and wandered in through the side door. I walked into the bar area. I noticed a few stern-looking men sitting at the bar who turned to look at me as I walked in. Judging by their demeanour, I had intruded into their space and certainly wasn't welcome. To my left I saw a stairwell next to the sign that said "Restaurant", so I took it as my cue to get out of there. Upstairs, while having my dinner in the restaurant, I felt a bit more relaxed to be away from the dodgy characters downstairs, though I did curse myself for once again being a bit foolish. I thought I had turned my back on that sort of behaviour when I cut back on my binge drinking, but I guess there were still parts of my personality I needed to iron out. Once I made it to the base of the stairwell, I made a dash for the safe confines of my hotel without once looking into the bar area. That was another close call.

I had one more free day before I had to meet up with my next Top Deck tour for dinner, so I decided to check out Kelly's Cellar. Built in March 1720, it is one of the oldest pubs in Belfast. It sits on a square beside Castle Court and it provided pub food and traditional music sessions. It sounded like my type of scene. I spent a few hours at Kelly's sampling the local ales and enjoying a nice feed. It was old-style, and I couldn't believe it was 300 years old! I imagined the things that must have taken place between those walls and all the characters who had frequented the place throughout history. After I had my full of beer, I heeded the trigger warnings with my binge drinking and got out of there. While walking back to my hotel I felt a sense of pride that I was in a place such as Ireland and I was still taking the positive steps to stay on top of the binge drinking. I was winning the battle. Once back in my room I decided to have an early night as I was due to meet up with the Top Deck group the following day. Like the last trip, I wondered who I would meet on this tour.

Around midday, I met up with the tour guide Emily and some of the tour group as we headed to the Belfast Peace Wall. The Peace Wall was built during the early years of The Troubles to separate the Republicans and nationalist Catholics from the predominantly loyalist and unionist Protestant neighbourhoods. People from all over the world had written on the wall and I also left a quote. I wrote, "Dreamers can never be tamed. Give peace a chance Belfast." I chatted to a few others on the tour to break the ice as, like my previous Top Deck tour, I was joining halfway through while different groups had already bonded. I remember chatting to a nice Canadian from Alberta, Deanna. Like Tonia and me the year before, she was also a solo traveller.

Three

Toowoomba Lads

That night I got ready and wandered down the street to the pub which was our designated meeting place for dinner. I ordered a beer and took a spot at the dinner table to wait for the rest of the group. Suddenly, this Aussie bloke came out of nowhere, sat down next to me and started chatting. His name was Lach Cowie, and he seemed like a bit of a character. Six other lads joined us, and I soon discovered that they were all great mates from Toowoomba travelling together. I was impressed albeit slightly envious they had the opportunity to travel together. They seemed to be having the time of their lives as I joined in and quickly got to know them all. Pat, Lachy and Dougal Evans, Turk, Dan and Ethan. I was enjoying myself but also felt a bit sad as I knew I would have fun with them if they were also on the tour.

The night would soon end which meant we would then go our separate ways. But to my surprise I soon found out they were on the tour. They had a big one the night before so didn't head out with the rest of the group for a visit to the Belfast Peace Wall earlier in the day. I was very happy to hear that as it called for another round of beers! After dinner we were all due to head downstairs to the basement bar for karaoke. I needed to go to the toilet first so I told the lads I would meet them down there shortly and to have a beer waiting for me. Once I got down to the bar though I couldn't find the lads anywhere. I kept searching for a familiar face from dinner but couldn't see one. "Have I been stood up?" That thought certainly washed over me. Oh well, I was at a karaoke bar in Ireland, so I decided to live it up instead of feeling too disappointed. However, no way was I singing karaoke. I kept an eye out though, but no one from the tour seemed to pop up in the bar. Man, I *have* been stood up by an entire Top Deck group I thought! After a few more beers I decided to call it a night and head back to the hotel. I woke up early and headed down to the lobby as we were due to depart for the Giant's Causeway. I met up with the rest of the tour group including the Toowoomba lads who were chatting about how much fun they had at the karaoke bar. "Hang on a minute," I replied. "I was at the karaoke bar, and I didn't see anyone there." Emily must have overheard and replied, "There are two karaoke bars downstairs." I must have gone to the wrong one. Even I had to have a bit of a chuckle at that as I hung my head in shame. "Who's the Goose." I was certainly back in tour mode and already making a name for myself. I heard Cowie had got up to sing Van Morrison's "Brown Eyed Girl" and I was even more disappointed I missed it. Cowie reminded me a lot of Shaban. Both outgoing and always up for a good time. As I was soon to discover, all the lads were up for a good time.

The Giant's Causeway was majestic and very scenic. By all accounts, it was a sign of what was to come on my journey through Ireland. Very scenic countryside. I wondered why the locals spent so much time in pubs when they had all these beautiful sights to explore, but then I was like that in my younger years, especially on my earlier trips. Come to think of it, a part of me still longed for that lifestyle, but I had to keep evolving. I was amazed by all the interlocking basalt columns, roughly 40,000 in total.

After spending the morning there, it was time to leave Northern Ireland for the Republic of Ireland as we headed for the harbour city of Galway. Straight away I found Galway to be a very lively place with plenty of traditional pubs, stone-clad cafes, boutiques and art galleries lining the winding lanes of the Latin Quarter. Portions of medieval city walls also surrounded us. I went for dinner with Emily and the Toowoomba lads. It was an enjoyable evening, and I got to know our tour guide and the lads a bit more.

The lads were taking turns telling drunken stories from their travels when Emily interrupted them to say, "Joel seems like a responsible traveller. I'm sure he doesn't want to listen to drunken stories all evening." I had a bit of a chuckle, and I remember thinking, "If only they knew." I must admit, it did make me feel good to think I was now a more responsible and mature traveller, and it was starting to come through with the people I met on my travels. Maybe I have come a long way since partying with the Brazilian chicks in Munich many years earlier. Good times. I couldn't afford to get too nostalgic though as I was travelling again which meant I now had plenty of new travel memories to make.

After dinner I checked out a few pubs with the lads before heading back to our hotel at a reasonable hour. The following morning, I decided to have a bit of a sleep-in instead of heading out early with the lads. I was already friends with a few of them on Facebook so I figured it would be easy to keep in touch. Pat had already sent me a message to let me know roughly their plans so we could meet up later. They had only just met me and were already happy to include me and invite me along for whatever they had planned. Shows what genuine people they were. I guess I was one of them for the time being.

Eventually I made it back down to the harbour for some more sightseeing. I then decided it was time to find a nice pub for lunch and a few beers. I *was* in Ireland after all, so I had plenty to pick from. I settled on Jury's Inn as it was in a good location and had a massive beer garden. Perfect setting for me. While relaxing in the beer garden having a beer I received a message on Facebook. It was from Pat to let me know they were heading to the Jury's Inn if I wanted to meet up with them there. Just as I finished reading the message, I looked up to see the Toowoomba lads walking into the beer garden. They couldn't believe it when they saw me sitting there. Talk about timing and being in the right place at the right time! I didn't even have to get up from my beer. For a bit of a joke, I replied to Pat's message as he sat down: "Ok, I'll meet you all there." Lol. It was an enjoyable afternoon and a great pub-crawl with the lads that night. As has been the story of my life, I didn't meet "my Galway girl" but I enjoyed my time there.

Four

ABERYSTWYTH, THE HIDDEN GEM

The next day was exciting and the part of the tour I had been looking forward to the most as we visited the majestic Cliffs of Moher which run 14km along the coast. They were breathtaking and well worth the visit. After that, we visited the Blarney Stone. No, I didn't kiss it – which is supposed to endow the kisser with the gift of the gab – but looking back, maybe I should have. Lol. While walking back to the bus, and despite the fact I was enjoying this trip and making new friends, I felt a wave of sadness wash over me as I thought about all the other friends I had made on my previous travels and wondered how they were all getting on. I guess I missed them now that I was travelling again.

Deanna often sat in the seat behind me on the bus and we would have a good chat while travelling between destinations as we struck up a friendship. We spent the next few days in Dublin checking out the sights such as Temple Bar and doing a tour of Guinness Storehouse. What could be more fun than hearing all about Ireland's famous brew along with tastings and a rooftop bar? I was in my element! One evening we all went out for dinner to watch an Irish skit. As expected, Cowie ended up being a part of the skit. As was often the case, I spent the rest of the night having a drinking session with the lads back at the hotel bar. I certainly was leaving no stone unturned, not only on this trip, but life in general.

After leaving the bright lights of Dublin, it was time to cross the channel on the ferry bound for Wales. I slept most of the journey. After visiting the town with the longest name in Wales, which I couldn't pronounce, we arrived in Aberystwyth which was to be our destination for the night. It was a university town situated on the coast of Wales. That evening in Aberystwyth I was to learn one of the most beautiful lessons of travelling. Maybe because it had been another full-on tour and I wasn't getting any younger, I decided not to head out with the lads that evening. Instead, I decided to have dinner at the hotel and an early night. Besides, we were heading to Cardiff the next day and I wanted to save myself for that.

I replied to Pat's usual message to let him know I was going to have a quiet one and he was cool with that. Not long after while checking out the dinner menu at the hotel bar, the lads came in for a quick beer before heading out. While chatting, I felt myself having a change of heart. I figured I had pushed myself to the limit every other tour I had been on, so why not do it once more seeing as we only had a few days to go? Besides, I may never get the chance to visit Aberystwyth again and it would be a hidden gem that I would miss out on seeing. As I mentioned earlier, I never leave any stone unturned. As I was about to discover, it would prove to be one of the best decisions I had ever made. One of the lads had searched online earlier and found a great place to eat. So, leading the way, we all followed him on a walk through the town. I obviously hadn't done my research on the town so imagine my surprise when we walked out of an alleyway to see the ocean in front of us. I hadn't realised we were on the coast. Even better, right in front of us was a pub with a massive pier out the back, stretching out over the ocean where you can really enjoy your beer while watching the sunset. I was in heaven. To think I almost missed out on all of this if I had stayed at the hotel. Champion – whichever of the lads who found this place. We walked out to the edge of the pier and sat at a few tables. The sunset was amazing as I got a photo with the lads. The sun was setting on another of my trips, so this was great to share that moment with the lads. It reminded me of the golden sunset I saw in Venice back in 2009. Aberystwyth was certainly a hidden gem as it ended up being a magical evening. Another travel memory that would stay with me for life.

Five

LONDON BOUND

After leaving the hidden gem of Aberystwyth, it was on to Cardiff which is the capital and largest city in Wales to spend the last few days of the tour. Seeing as I hadn't planned or booked any accommodation for my time in the UK, I decided to give sightseeing with the lads a miss to jump online and start booking accommodation so I wouldn't be stranded when we arrived in London in a few days' time. I had been in touch with Richard and planned to head out to Guildford to catch up and stay with him for a few days, so I only had to book something for one night in London and the week following my few days in Guildford. I hadn't heard from Shaun but discovered on my previous trips he always seemed to get in touch at just the right moment, so I was confident I would catch up with him as well.

I ended up booking a hotel in central London for the Sunday night while I booked a place out near Hyde Park for the week following Guildford. I was also in touch with Emily from Stratford and planned to also head up there to spend a few days, so I kept my last week in the UK open until we worked out suitable dates. I was now all set.

That night I headed out with the lads and the rest of the tour group for our last night together to celebrate. After dinner we went to a nightclub not too far from our hotel. I have already mentioned how I feel about nightclubs but seeing as it was our last night together and the lads being younger and keen, I decided to join them for a few. I was on the right track with my binge drinking but if anything was going to be a test to see how far I had come, then this was it! The lads were keen to get into it – being younger I figured they either hadn't developed a binge drinking problem or were just unaware if they had one! I, on the other hand, had to play it safe.

After a few rounds of beers, the shots came out and that is when the alarm bells started going off in my mind, so I decided to make my getaway. I told Cowie and seeing as I had opened up to him on the tour about my history with binge drinking, he totally understood. He even offered to walk with me back to the hotel to make sure I got back safe. What a champion. Once I was back in my room and Cowie had left to head back to the nightclub, I reminisced about my travels in cities all over the world. I couldn't remember getting back to my hotel after a drunken night out but now I had seemingly overcome my binge drinking problem and was playing it safe I had someone making sure I got back to my hotel safe and sound. Life can be ironic at times. Haha.

Six

ANOTHER HARD GOODBYE

The next morning we all gathered in the lobby for the final leg of the journey to London with a stop at Stonehenge. While listening to the lads tell stories of their drunken escapades from the night before I felt a little envious but happy I was putting myself in these situations and staying strong and not falling into bad habits. I was holding firm. I was winning. Stonehenge was impressive –another famous landmark to tick off the list. I wandered the grounds chatting with Cowie.

We arrived back in London in the evening and once again I felt that feeling start to surface where I was about to say goodbye to more people I had grown fond of on my travels. Obviously, the lads, but also our tour guide Emily and my new friend Deanna. I got a good photo with Emily and the lads in front of the hotel then said my goodbyes. Seeing as the lads were based in Australia, I felt I would get a chance to catch up with them again on my travels over coming years, and that feeling would prove to be correct.

After saying our goodbyes I caught a taxi to my hotel. I knew London was a big place, but it was taking ages to arrive at my destination. I questioned the taxi driver, and he said that due to roadworks he had to take a longer route. Deep in my heart I knew that wasn't the case, but I was too tired and being the nice guy that I was, I decided not to make a big thing of it and just hoped for the best. He eventually dropped me off at the hotel where; after getting to my room, I finally fell into a deep sleep.

I woke up the next morning feeling a bit under the weather as I had caught a bad dose of the flu. But I was so looking forward to seeing Richard and hopefully Shaun again, so I had to push through. I caught the train out to Guildford where Richard was waiting at the station. It was great seeing him again. The last time was when I first met him with Shaun during my travels through the UK and Scandinavia a few years earlier.

After dropping my stuff off at his place we went for a walk along the main river that runs through Guildford, then went for a few pints at Richard's local. Almost as if on cue, Shaun sent me a message to see where I was. That guy is very intuitive and must have sensed I was in Guildford. We met up with him for dinner at a hummus restaurant and the conversation just flowed. Shaun touched on some of the stories from his time in America and once again I was intrigued.

Afterwards the three of us went for another walk around Guildford, and after planning to meet up with Shaun for breakfast, Richard and I headed back to his place. Richard's apartment was on the second floor and through his window you could oversee a bit of Guildford. We sat in his loungeroom and spoke throughout the night. Richard opened up to me about some of the trials and tribulations he had been through in his life, and it made me think that what happened with myself and Marcia wasn't that big a deal. But another thing I have learned about life is we all have different experiences, and if something we go through does hurt there is a reason, and if we are prepared to search it is an opportunity to heal and grow as a person.

Seven

Time to Heal and Grow

Talking to Richard that night was very therapeutic and made me see things from a different perspective. Richard had a few things to do in the morning so couldn't come to breakfast with Shaun and me. While chatting, I told him a bit more about my life when suddenly out of the blue Shaun asked what time Richard was giving me a lift back to London. I told him about lunchtime, and he asked if I was interested in heading back to his apartment to do a podcast and interview about my life. Shaun had such a big following in the UK and around the world with his online podcasts. I couldn't believe my luck! My story would get out there now.

We went back to his place where I watched Shaun set it all up. We then sat on the couch with the camera rolling as Shaun interviewed me about my life. It was unreal. Once we finished, he told me it would be uploaded to YouTube within the hour. Wow! What an experience! Once I arrived back at Richard's, I told him all about it and he smiled and said he had a feeling Shaun would do something like that as he was always thinking big, and my story was certainly inspiring. Richard drove me back to London around midday as he was planning on meeting up with his friend Roger for a few beers at his local pub. Roger was in his 60s and an Aussie who had been living in the UK for 30-plus years, so it sounded like he had seen a lot of life.

Richard thought it would be great for me to meet him. Roger was a character with plenty of stories to tell. I was in my element with all the storytelling. I finally said goodbye to Richard and Roger and caught a taxi to check into my hotel near Hyde Park. We drove through the park, and I was amazed by the sheer size of it. I knew then I would be going for a stroll to take it all in during my stay in the area.

The hotel was another of those old-style London hotels I had become accustomed to. It was all about the experience. To get to my room on the top floor I had to walk up a massive staircase. "At least I would get fit on this trip," I thought. The room was more like a loft which I was okay with. I was still feeling the effects of the flu, so I was keen to rest up for a bit. While relaxing in my room Shaun sent me a message to let me know he had just uploaded our podcast onto YouTube. I was very excited to hear that as Shaun had a massive following on his YouTube channel. This was sure to get my story out there even further. I also shared it on my Facebook page and seeing as I have always loved quotes, I figured the perfect quote to title the podcast would be from kung fu legend Bruce Lee: "Don't pray for an easy life, pray for the strength to endure a tough one." Perfect.

I was also hoping to catch up with some other friends while I was in the UK so while resting up with the flu I decided to start planning a few things. I got in touch with Emily and planned to head to Stratford-upon-Avon that Friday until Tuesday, so I booked my accommodation and train ticket. I planned to catch up with Emily on the Monday so that was all set. I was heading to Shakespeare country, and I was eager to explore more of the UK. I was also in touch with Alicia who was still based in London. We planned to meet up for a few drinks at a place called Boxpark Shoreditch on Wednesday evening. Claire, my old school friend, was out of town again.

Eight

WHITE NINJA

The following day I felt better so went for a walk-through Hyde Park. It was beautiful and I just couldn't believe how big it was. It reminded me of Central Park in New York. I also discovered a lot of famous artists have concerts in the park. The river running through the middle also added to the scenery. Bliss. I was relishing the chance to explore the outer suburbs of London.

Soho was also within walking distance of my hotel, so I also went for a few walks to spend some time there. Soho is one of my favourite places in London. Will always have fond memories of catching up with my old school friend Claire for dinner while there in 2017. Going for a stroll through Soho and taking in the vibe is a relaxant for me

On the Wednesday evening, I got ready and caught the subway out to Shoreditch for my catch up with Alicia. Boxpark was an old shipping container storage area which has now been re-purposed as a pop-up mall with plenty of cafés. Alicia was running a little late, so I ordered myself a beer and waited at our designated meeting place. She finally arrived and we settled into a great evening of catching up. We spoke of old times and mutual friends back in Harvey while the drinks flowed. We also had a laugh from when we randomly crossed paths at Heathrow during my visit to London the previous year. What were the odds of that happening? I found Boxpark Shoreditch to be a lively environment. It was another enjoyable evening as it was great catching up with Alicia again. Besides Claire, I had now caught up with the people I was hoping to catch up with on this visit and it was time to start focussing on my journey up to Stratford-upon-Avon for the weekend.

I checked out of my old-style hotel loft Friday morning and headed for the train station. It was a two-hour train ride and as usual, I spent it staring out the window at the lush green English countryside. Once I arrived at the train station in Stratford, instead of my usual routine of getting a cab, I decided to search for my hotel on foot so I could start exploring the town straight away. Stratford-upon-Avon is a medieval market town located in England's West Midlands. As the name suggests, the river Avon runs through the town. I was staying at the Crowne Plaza which, as I was soon to discover, was located not too far from the banks of the Avon.

That evening after checking into my room, I went for another stroll. The town had a bohemian feel to it, and I felt at ease like I had just discovered another hidden gem. Oh, the joys of travelling. I was also overjoyed to see Stratford had its very own mini-London Eye. Maybe it was my own small-town background coming out, but it kind of felt like home, especially chatting to the locals at the pub while having dinner. I wasn't planning to catch up with Emily until Monday as she was a bit busy. I decided to make the most of the weekend by doing the tourist thing.

Seeing as I was in the birthplace and home of William Shakespeare, I decided to follow the trail of the famous poet and playwright. As a traveller in the 21st century I was now using my phone as a map. I checked out Shakespeare's birthplace and childhood home, the school he went to and later during a hop on hop off bus tour, I was also able to visit his house and Anne Hathaway's Cottage – a bit of history which made the town a popular tourist destination as I soaked it all up. I found the town also had a bit of a city feeling about it which I found refreshing. Plenty of pubs, but I certainly wasn't falling back into temptation. Just a few quiet beers, here and there.

I had always loved visiting pubs wherever I travelled, and that hadn't changed. I was now aware of my binge drinking habit and I was keeping that in check and under control. I was now becoming a bit of an expert, knowing when to sneak away instead of hanging around and having that one beer too many. To all you people I ended up drinking with at the pubs during that trip who wondered why I didn't return after going to the toilet or heading outside for a smoke, now you know why. Lol. Nothing personal. I just couldn't risk putting myself in a position where I would drink too much. I'm pretty sure that happened at least a couple of times during that weekend in Stratford. I was becoming the "White Ninja". Now you see me – now you don't. Disappeared in a cloud of smoke. Haha. By the time the people I was drinking with realised I wasn't coming back from my toilet break, often I would be back at my hotel safely tucked up in bed.

Nine

An English Rose

I woke up on Monday morning with an anxious but excited feeling. I had enjoyed the experience in Stratford so far, but catching up with Emily was the main reason that brought me here. As I mentioned in my first book, I met Emily at Eden nightclub during a night out on my Top Deck tour through Spain the previous year. We got chatting, stayed in touch and now we were about to catch up again in her hometown of Stratford.

Emily had to work in the morning, so we planned to meet at the clock tower in town, just after midday. It was no Big Ben, but I managed to find the tower quite easily. As usual, I arrived at our meeting spot a little early, so I decided to get a cheeky beer in while I waited. As if on cue, I spied a pub across from the clock tower which had a seating area out the front. Perfect place to wait.

While relaxing out the front with a beer, I thought about how similar this experience felt to waiting for Marcia during our catch up in Toronto six years earlier. This time, I was waiting for an English Rose. Not only was I still good friends with people I grew up with from back home, but I had also now made friends on my travels and been lucky enough to catch up with quite a few of them again in different parts of the world

I thought about those long, lonely nights I spent sitting in my car at Myalup Beach after PJ died and how I have gone on to create friendships all over the world. In a sense, I was able to create my own destiny

I suddenly noticed someone wandering aimlessly around near the clock tower like she was looking for someone or something. Emily had arrived and she was obviously looking for me, so I had one last sip of my beer and wandered over to greet her. After the warm embrace she asked me what I felt like doing? I suggested she could show me a bit more around her hometown. She liked that idea, so we went for stroll down towards the riverbanks to check out Bancroft Park. We then visited a butterfly farm that was situated in the park. So far it had been another enjoyable day, but little did I know I was just about to get a huge fright!

As a self-proclaimed arachnophobe, nothing scares me more than spiders! They really freak me out. I was observing all the butterflies darting around my face when Emily pointed towards the wall and casually said, "Look at the tarantula behind the glass!" "Oh okay. I will…you said what!!!?" I froze and looked at Emily to see if she was serious. "It's only a spider," she replied. "Yeah, a very big spider," I said. I couldn't move and Emily started cracking up laughing. I don't think she had met anyone more scared of spiders than me. But I guess we all must face – and somehow overcome – our fears at some stage so I figured, why not today, and while in the company of an English rose.

When I finally regained my composure, I tiptoed towards the glass and peeked through. This thing was a monster! Just like a massive hairy human hand. I gulped at the thought of it crawling over me. "How strong was that glass?" I wondered. I took a pic of Emily posing next to it, as casual as ever. "Were we seeing the same thing," I wondered. Her reaction was the complete opposite to mine. I finally convinced her we'd better leave before it became adventurous and got out! That was another close call, but I was getting used to them by now. We then went for a late lunch at a café in town. While chatting I got to know more about Emily and her interests. She also loved travelling and was studying to become a veterinarian because she loved animals. She was a lovely person and easy to chat to. Afterwards, we went for one last walk through the town before it came time to say goodbye. By now, it seemed I was forever catching up with and then saying goodbye to friends all over the world. It was becoming emotionally draining, though in a positive way, as I found it was the time spent together and memories you take away with you that are important. Family, friends and memories are most valuable in this world. Everything else is just temporary. It was good seeing Emily again in her hometown, and as I went out for dinner that night, I had a warm feeling in my heart. It was a great finish to my time in Stratford.

Ten

Amsterdam, Here I Come!

Later that night, I jumped online to book accommodation for my last few nights in London and my week in Amsterdam. The thought of heading back to Amsterdam was getting me excited! It would be my fourth visit now and I wondered what adventures (or misadventures) awaited me this time? I guess I would soon find out. Even better, I was planning on catching up with my friend Rarni in Amsterdam.

I first met Rarni back in Western Australia on a night out with Luke down south in Dunsborough back in 2007. She was in her early 20s and living down there. She had moved around a lot but always kept finding herself back in Dunsborough, so I guess it felt like home to her. And who could blame her? Such a great lifestyle down that way. Lots of sun, surf and relaxing at good ol' "Dunsborough".

We kept in touch over the years and caught up whenever we found ourselves in the same part of the world, which for two "wanderers" like us, wasn't too often. But it was always great when we did, so you can imagine my surprise when Rarni sent me a message after I put a post on Facebook with my impending travel plans to find out what dates I would be travelling as she was planning a trip to Europe mid-year. As luck would have it, our plans fell together nicely as Rarni was due to land in Amsterdam a few days before I flew home, so it was all set. Thank you, universe!

I caught the train from Stratford back to London, checked into my hotel and started preparing for the last stage of my journey. But seriously, how do you really prepare for Amsterdam? I was boosting! I caught a taxi from the airport to within walking distance of my hotel, my usual routine. Back walking these narrow streets and crossing bridges over the canals always seem to do something to my senses. There is no place in the world quite like Amsterdam! You don't even have to be stoned to feel like you're in a haze. I found trying to find my hotel – even if I was going the wrong way – to also be a pleasant experience as I floated through the haze. Bliss.

I finally floated into a bar to ask for directions. A Pommy guy sitting there gave me directions to my hotel which I was happy to hear was only just around the corner and a few blocks away. I thanked him and continued on my blissful way. Little did I know it then, but not only would I see that Pommy guy again, but we would share some good times and hazy evenings over the week I was there. That first night I was tame. I just went out for dinner and thought about how I was going to make the most of my time in Amsterdam. Seeing as it was now my fourth visit there, I decided nothing would be off limits, besides getting black-out drunk of course! I had already identified that as being a problem, and after all the positive steps I had taken to overcome it, even being back in Amsterdam wasn't going to tempt me to fall back down that dark hole! I was staying strong on that front.

Eleven

SHOOTING STARS AND EXTRATERRESTRIALS

When it came to drugs however, I was only really a dabbler. Every once in a blue moon during my younger years, if it felt right and the opportunity presented itself, I would dabble and take something to see what the experience felt like. You would have read some of those experiences in my first book. They were often hit and miss. Haha. But I had never taken drugs constantly enough to develop a habit or become an addict, and by this stage in my life they had pretty much become non-existent for me. But when it came to Amsterdam, I was wiling to make an exception. If it was sold over the counter legally and it felt right, I was willing to try anything. I rubbed my hands together with glee. What a fun-filled week this was shaping up to be!

Over the coming days, I pretty much stuck to the same routine. Mid-morning I would walk from my hotel into Dam Square and the red-light district, do a spot of window shopping and enjoy a mini pub crawl. On one of those days, while walking back to my hotel, I passed the bar on the corner where I had asked for directions that first day and decided to pop in for a quiet beer. Lo and behold, who was sitting at the exact same spot? None other than the Pommy guy who helped me with directions a few days earlier. He seemed friendly, so naturally I joined him for a few beers to get to know him better. His name was Chris and worked as a sports coach at a college back home in the UK. He also enjoyed playing golf and, like most people in the UK, Amsterdam seemed to be his choice of destination whenever he wanted to get away for a while. This bar was obviously his local drinking spot – I guess it was mine now as well. Perfect location, just around the corner from my hotel.

The following day I popped in again as I knew Chris would be there. This time I was feeling a bit more adventurous and up for some excitement so after a few beers I excused myself and ducked into a convenience store not far from the bar. I bought myself a bag of magic mushrooms and I gobbled them down pretty much as soon as I stepped back outside! Arrgghh! They tasted horrible, but I guess I wasn't taking them for the taste! Now, I was ready for a mission! I joined Chris back at the bar and for a while nothing happened. Then, suddenly, it just hit me out of nowhere! Just like what happened in my hotel on my last visit when I tried magic mushrooms, I felt my mind go into another galaxy!

I went outside, sat in one of the chairs out the front and lit up a smoke. I leaned back and looked up at the sky. It was now nighttime, but the sky was lit up with what looked to me like shooting stars. They were everywhere! Some even shot straight past my head! I had to sway a little so they wouldn't hit me! Wow! This was intense! I suddenly heard these strange noises all around me. So, I looked around at the different groups of people chatting, but they didn't sound like humans, they sounded more like aliens! Was I surrounded by extra-terrestrials disguised as humans? Surely not. This seemed a little far-fetched, even for Amsterdam! I was freaking out a bit though, so I decided to wander up close to each group to make sure I was hearing right. What I discovered was when I got close to people, they went back to sounding like humans, but when I put a bit of distance between us, they sounded like aliens! This was doing my head in!

I decided to find a safe place, so I went back inside and sat down on the stool right next to Chris. Luckily, there was very little distance between us, so when he spoke, he sounded human, and I could understand him!

Now Chris had experienced life, so it didn't take him long to realise that we were now in different worlds and the world I frequented was way, way out there! But Chris had taken a liking to me and being the champion he is, he didn't leave me stranded. He was going to stick by me on my mission. He ordered us both another beer and asked where I parked my spaceship! I told him I'm pretty sure I'm still coming into land! The barmaids overheard the conversation and didn't even flinch! Being in Amsterdam they had obviously heard similar or even weirder conversations!

Chris was one of those guys who could make you laugh easy, so being in his company really helped me through even though I was still hallucinating pretty bad. Even more so, when a small black cat jumped up on the bar and the barmaids started fussing over it – it had me wondering, was that real or was I just seeing things? Chris was a man of routine so, at a certain time, he finished his last beer and headed back to his hotel. I stayed for a few more as I wasn't ready just yet to face the four walls of my hotel room in the state I was in. After a while, I decided to do the same.

While walking back I noticed the shooting stars had gone and the groups of people I passed seemed to be chatting normally, so the effects of the mushrooms had pretty much worn off. I should have realised that when I looked around to see if I did park my spaceship outside the pub, but now it was nowhere to be ssen!

I woke up the next morning feeling a little scattered and lightheaded. "Those magic mushrooms can sure take it out of you," I thought, as I scratched my head. Everything seemed a little hazier on my walk into Dam Square that morning. The sounds of Amsterdam were ringing through my good ear. Oh Amsterdam! When I popped in to have a beer with Chris later that evening he quipped, "How did you get here? Did you walk or fly the spaceship?" I had a laugh and replied, "Nah. No big missions for me tonight. Just a few quiet beers."

Twelve

High on Life and Friendships

I felt fresh the next day, so I had more of a spring in my step as I made my way into Dam Square. I decided to do a little more sightseeing to start things off. Emily from Stratford had sent me a message to let me know Body Worlds, a science museum in Amsterdam, was worth checking out so I did. I followed that with a beer at an ice bar, dressed like an Eskimo, that was certainly an experience!

After that I went for a late lunch and a few beers at The Flying Pig, a well-known pub in Amsterdam. I was feeling on top of the world!

While sitting there I received a message from Rarni to remind me she was flying in the next day and she, with one of her Dutch friends, could meet at my hotel lobby around 3pm. I liked that idea! I was feeling pretty good by the time I popped in for a few beers with Chris that evening! I knew I would be feeling even better shortly! After a few beers I again ducked over to the convenience store. This time, instead of going for the hallucinogens, I was after a more euphoric high, so I purchased a tube of liquid ecstasy. To play it safe, I skolled half and saved the other half for later. I wanted to take it slow and see how it affected me first. But to my dismay, after about an hour of sitting back in the bar with Chris, I had hardly felt anything at all. So, I did what any other adventurous, thrill-seeking, risk-taking individual would do – I skolled the other half! Sure enough the high soon hit me.

I was floating in a euphoric state I had never reached before. I had to keep a firm grip on the bar to keep myself from floating away all together! I had the biggest smile on my face as I looked around at all the beautiful people in the bar just waiting for me to strike up a friendship with them. Even though I had only just met him, in that moment, Chris was the best person in the world! His jokes were funnier and everything he said was pure wisdom. I then decided that I needed to share the love with everyone at the bar that night instead of just Chris. So, I started floating up to random strangers and chatting like we had known each other forever. Luckily for me everyone I spoke to seemed happy and willing to have a chat with me. I seem to have a likeable personality as demonstrated by all the friends I had made in my life, but now, more than ever, I needed that trait to shine through as I navigated my way through the high I was experiencing.

That likeable trait must have been shining like a beacon as I was on a roll and making friends with everyone. Every so often I would call Chris over from his spot at the bar to also meet my new friends and he would happily oblige. At the designated time, Chris finished his last beer and left. I thought, "What a beautiful person, always sticking to his routine." The bar eventually closed, and I lingered out the front chatting to anyone and everyone until I ended up being the last one there.

I wondered what to do next as my night was a long way from being over, even if it was well past the midnight hour. I wasn't going to be sleeping anytime soon, so I figured if I searched hard enough surely, I would find a bar that's still open. So off I went, power walking through the narrow streets and over the bridges just searching for anything to keep the night going. I was about to give up when I saw a light up ahead. I ran up to it, and to my great delight, it was a bar. I went inside to find it empty, except for a guy working behind the bar. He said they closed at 4am, which was still roughly an hour away, and that suited me just fine. So, I ordered a beer took a spot at the bar and proceeded to tell him my life story. Oh, the joys of being high on ecstasy at 3am in the morning, in Amsterdam. To his credit, he didn't seem annoyed, but rather intrigued and inspired by the stories of my life.

At closing time, I started walking back to my hotel. The sun was starting to rise, and I thought how peaceful and beautiful Amsterdam felt in the early morning light. I could feel myself starting to come down off my high, but even though sleep was still an hour or so away, I decided to go back to my room to rest up so I could be right for when Rarni and her friend arrived at 3pm that afternoon.

After a few hours' sleep I felt somewhat okay so got ready and headed down to the lobby. I decided to have a beer at the hotel bar while I waited which brought me back to a good level. Rarni finally arrived and it was great to see her because even though we had always kept in touch I was pretty sure it had been eight or so years since we last caught up. Even better, this reunion was taking place in Amsterdam! She introduced me to her friend Nils, then the three of us left the hotel to experience all that Amsterdam had to offer! Come to think of it, I had probably already done that, but I was willing to give it one last hurrah for Rarni's sake.

We found an Aussie bar not far from my hotel where we commenced what would become an enjoyable evening. Rarni and I had plenty to catch up on and Nils seemed like a nice guy. He was Dutch and local so he could show us all the hidden gems in the city. That is exactly what he did as we ended up checking out the university and one of the popular museums. We finished up the night at the bars in the red-light district, but that was always going to happen. All up, it was another enjoyable night and great catch-up with my old friend.

I woke up the following morning with that familiar feeling I had become accustomed to when I knew another trip was coming to an end as I was due to fly home the next day. I spent those last few days doing my usual bout of soul searching and reflection, just wandering around Amsterdam with a clear mind. I could hear birds chirping in the distance as I took it all in one last time. I thought about how far I had come from the early days of being an anxious and nervous traveller where I was lucky enough to have good friends such as PJ, Adam, Jono, Crudder, Luke and even Dad to travel with while I was finding my feet to where I was now – a confident, solo traveller. I had certainly come a long way.

PJ would be proud, I thought, as I felt a few tears well up in my eyes. I also had that strange but familiar feeling I felt while walking the streets of Toronto with Adam and Flemo during my last visit back in 2012, a feeling that I may not be back for a while – so "take it all in mate", I said to myself. We were still more than a year and half from Covid impacting the world, but obviously I didn't know that then. Maybe the universe was telling me something, subconsciously.

Thirteen

Home Time

I packed and headed for the airport. I didn't get a chance to see Chris again before he went back to the UK, but we were now friends on Facebook so, like many others I had met on my travels, I was confident we would keep in touch. I enjoyed the time I spent with him in Amsterdam and I'm pretty sure he saw me as a bit of a character. Lol.

As was often the case, I continued my soul searching on the long flight back to WA. I was content with where I was now as a traveller. Even though what happened between Marcia and I sent me to a bit of a dark place and left me feeling lost, I was able to take the steps to look deeper into myself to bounce back, and to go on three more overseas trips was meaningful.

I was able to rediscover my love of travelling and flying again. I also noticed the progress I had made during the three trips. During the first trip to the UK, Iceland and Scandinavia, I sometimes struggled with travelling solo, but I felt I was able to come into myself more as a solo traveller on my next two trips to Spain and Ireland. I was really looking forward to doing more travelling over the coming years, but unbeknownst to me this would be my last overseas trip for a while. Over the coming years something huge worldwide was about to occur that would sadly prevent me from travelling overseas. Until then, it was back home and getting on with life.

Fourteen

The Snowball Effect

It was now mid-2018 and things were happening. I was becoming more aware of the importance of keeping a positive outlook as it can influence the direction your life takes subconsciously. I really felt that. I still had my house and investment property in Myalup, so I was set up in life. My brothers were also going well. Frog was busy with his young family while Kelvin had come a long way since turning his life around and was achieving some good things. He had his own local radio segment a well as organising and promoting music festivals around Bunbury which I often went to as a show of support. Mum and Dad, as always, were happy and supportive of us all.

Even though I had now come into my own as a solo and confident traveller, the most positive thing happening in my life at that time was the steps I was taking to share my story. Doors were continuing to open for me as I gathered more momentum. Not long after my solo trip I was invited to give a speech to the students at St Anne's School in Harvey. This was big for me as they were growing up in the same community as I had. By this stage I had decided to put heaps of photos of my life and travels onto a USB and use it as a slideshow which would be set up behind me to give more depth to my presentations. The children at St Anne's that day loved my speech and were very engaging when I took questions afterwards. They also couldn't believe I knew a lot of their parents! Good chance I also partied with their parents back in the day, but the kids didn't have to know that bit! Haha.

To make a positive day even better, my friend Coralee worked at St Anne's, so it was great to see her too. With me off travelling the world and Coralee busy raising a family, it had been a few years since we last saw one another before that day. Like all my good friends, it was just like no time had passed at all, and we picked up where we left off and had a great catch up. After losing myself out there in this crazy world, and now I was starting to find my way back it was a blessing to have friends I grew up with such as Coralee still in my life, and they will always be there for me and continue to have my best interests at heart. At that stage, I probably needed to gravitate back to those friendships to gain some support and strength.

After catching up again that day at St Anne's, I knew it wouldn't be long before Coralee and I would catch up for a coffee in town. Family and good friends will always be the wind beneath my wings.

Following the success of my talk at St Anne's, a lady reached out to see if I wouldn't mind doing a speech for the children at a primary school in Donnybrook. Her name was Tamara and she was a teacher there. The snowball effect was obviously playing a part in my life as my story seemed to be spreading. Donnybrook was out of my comfort zone of Harvey and Bunbury but would be beneficial to my growth as a public speaker. So, early one day in August, I drove to Donnybrook and had a quick look around the town before my speech at the school. I remember visiting Donnybrook a few times with Nanna and my cousins as a kid to check out the Big Apple, so it was nice to be back again all those years later. Tamara was lovely and I ended up doing three speeches there to different classes that day. Like at St Anne's, the children took a lot away from my story and were very engaging with questions afterwards. However, I was very relieved the children didn't ask questions about Amsterdam and what I got up to there, as that part of my life was strictly for adults only! Haha.

Even in these early stages of getting my story out there, I pretty much went with the same theme I often use for my talks at schools – overcoming adversity, developing resilience, treating one another with kindness and compassion and, of course, no bullying! I often touched on the theme of bullying by describing my own experiences of never really encountering it. I was quite popular amongst my school peers, but if it had been different this could have really impacted my life in a negative way. The children seemed touched and inspired by my story, so I now knew I was making a difference, especially with the younger generations.

Around that time another friend I went to school with, Sharon, also reached out to see if I would be happy to chat to her students at Carey Baptist College in Perth. Indeed I was. I felt blessed having all these contacts which presented me with opportunities while I was finding my feet as a public speaker. Seeing as the speech was planned for a Monday, I went up at the weekend and stayed at Adam and Nancy's place who were still happily based in Perth.

Life seems to get busier as we get older, so whenever I have a public speaking engagement or other event in Perth, I usually plan to catch up and spend time with Adam and Nancy – not many things more valuable in life than family, good friends, time and memories. This was another good friendship that has stood the test of time. All up, it was another great weekend and successful speech.

Fifteen

Tragedy Strikes

Life seemed to be going well as I had gained quite a bit of happiness and positivity back. But then, just after Christmas 2018, tragedy struck our family once again. My brother Frog first met Cara around 2006, and they immediately formed a great friendship. Between myself and my two brothers, we had never had any trouble making friendships, and we all had a big circle of friends. Mum and Dad, being the people they are, always accepted and liked our friends as if they were part of the family. A friend of ours was a friend of theirs. Frog and Cara created such a special bond and friendship like they were two sides of a coin. She became one of his best friends, certainly his closest female friend, and, in turn, our family embraced her. Also, at a time when she felt she needed a change of scenery, she moved interstate and lived with Frog and Michayla in Melbourne while they were there. Cara was also great friends with Michayla and between the three of them they had a special bond. So many beautiful memories shared together.

I remember before they moved to Melbourne while I was still living at Frog's, Cara was over having drinks. I brought up the topic of the book I was currently writing on my life and Cara wanted to see it. So, I showed her what I had already written and straight away she was interested and intrigued by it. For the rest of the night, she kept asking questions, and whenever I saw her after that she would ask how it was coming along and to hurry up and get it published as she couldn't wait to read it and have a copy in her hands.

Sadly, she never got that chance. Towards the end of 2018 she moved in with friends in Perth as she was studying to become a nurse. They had a place in the outer suburbs which, being a country girl at heart, suited Cara. By all accounts, she was happy as it seemed she had found her niche in life. Tragically, a few days after Christmas 2018, Cara was home alone around midday when an intruder broke in and, in an act of senseless violence, Cara was killed by a stranger. Cara was such a beautiful soul who was loved by everyone who had the pleasure of meeting her. So many people were impacted by her sudden passing. She radiated light and compassion wherever she went which drew people in. She wanted to help people which was evident with the studying and training for a career she was passionate about at the time of her passing. Cara also loved sunflowers which was reflective of her personality. She will certainly live on in the hearts and memories of everyone who knew and loved her. This second book is dedicated to Cara. Shine on beautiful diamond.

Sixteen

LIFE BEGINS AT 40

Though things would never be the same for those who knew Cara best, life had to go on, and early in 2019 I celebrated another great milestone as I turned 40. They say life begins at 40, so that gave me a bit of optimism, but it also left me wondering, "How could it top the life I had already led?" I guess I was eager to find out. I now had found my purpose and vision in life, so the path ahead for me seemed a lot clearer now.

I celebrated my 40th with family and friends at the Old Coast Road Brewery which is located not far from Myalup. It was a great day. Adam was working away at the time so he and Nancy couldn't make it, and some other friends also had prior commitments, but it was still a good turnout. Frog also had to work, but Michayla came along. Mum, Dad, Nanna, Kelvin, Normie and Leanne, Mark and Liz, Ken and Katie, Calvin, Ash and many other friends turned up to help me celebrate. Kelvin arranged for two of his mates to play live music as a two-piece. I knew Renee and Rooboy from partying with the Binningup crew back in the day, so they were also there. Rooboy, being the character he is, decided after a few drinks to join in with the band! Unfortunately, they had no drum kit set up, but that wasn't a problem for Rooboy as he gathered up some pots and pans and other utensils to make his own drum kit! The band now became a three-piece with a drummer! In the spirit of the evening, he sounded pretty good and as soon as I heard the sound of the pots and pans echoing through the air, I immediately jumped up onto a chair and started dancing. I guess you could say my 40s had started off with a bang! Lol. All up, it was another enjoyable evening. Not long after my 40th, Justin Rake once again reached out to see if I was interested in doing a follow up of my life story for the paper. It was now going on four years since we did the first article, so I figured the timing was perfect for a follow-up. Justin was now working for the *Mandurah Mail* which gave my story more potential reach. So, we caught up, did the interview and when it came out in both the *Bunbury Mail* and the *Mandurah Mail,* I was happy as I felt Justin did another great job with the update to my story. Even better, it was Ken's 40th the same night I did the interview which gave me even more reason to celebrate! Boosting! It was almost that time for me to start planning my travels for the year. I did a bit of thinking about where I wanted to go and decided I would like to experience something different this time. Having already seen and experienced so much overseas, I suddenly realised I had seen and experienced very little of Australia, which is home. Maybe it was time to explore more of my own backyard. What swayed my thinking even further was out of all the friendships and contacts I had made on my travels over the years, most of them seemed to reside on the east coast of Australia. It also helped that Luke was now based in Geelong while Caliopi was based in Hepburn Springs, a small town located in the Daylesford area in country Victoria. I figured I could explore the east coast while catching up with friends along the way. Win-win situation. So, I started reaching out to my friends over east and they were all keen to catch up with me.

Shaban was still living a few hours out of Melbourne, while friends I had made on my latest travels, like Tonia, were in Sydney. Then there were the lads from Toowoomba. Aaron and Rachel, who I met during Contiki 2014 in the US with Luke, were also based in Sydney. My old friend Louisa and Adrian lived there too. Wow, what a great trip I had in front of me. Luke even offered to pick me up from the airport once I arrived at my first destination which was Melbourne. It was now 20 years since I first visited Sydney on that mystery flight with PJ, so it was only fitting I was going back for another visit. Quite emotional. I planned to fly out during the first week in May.

Luckily, I didn't book my flight straight away as I received an invite to Calvin's 40th at Ascot that weekend. I rubbed my hands together with glee – I can start catching up with friends before I had even left the state – what an awesome start to my trip that would be!

Even though I was planning to travel to three states, I knew the main state I would be in during my trip would be mildly drunk so I figured Calvin's 40th would be a perfect start to proceedings. Plus, Calvin made it to my 40th earlier in the year, so I was never going to miss celebrating it with my great mate.

I booked my flight for the Sunday and hoped my hangover wasn't going to be too bad. I booked two nights at the Great Eastern Motor Lodge Hotel in Perth, and I was all set. Mum loves the casino and any excuse for a visit would do, so she offered to drive me up. I also booked a room for Mum at the lodge. I was packed and ready to go, so once I had finished work on the Friday, Mum drove us up to Perth where we checked into the hotel. We went out and had Chinese for dinner, then, seeing I had a big month in front of me, decided to have an early night.

I rose early and went to the casino with Mum for breakfast. Afterwards, Mum went to try her luck on the pokie machines while I headed back to the hotel to get ready. Adam knew I was in Perth for the 40th so he phoned to let me know he was on his way to pick me up from the hotel to head out for lunch at a pub. I liked that idea so the catch up with friends was well and truly underway. After a feed and a quiet beer, Adam dropped me off at Ascot Racecourse as I was in the mood to start celebrating Calvin's 40th. Calvin had booked a bar for his function, so I found it and started mingling straight away. I caught up with plenty of familiar faces. I was not a big fan of horse racing, but if there was beer and plenty of people to chat with, I was in my element. It was a great day and that night we all headed to the casino to continue the celebrations. I was in the mood, but also sticking to the mid-strength beer and being aware of the level of intoxication I was at. Around 10.30pm and while most of the revellers were on the dancefloor, I decided to do the "White Ninja" so I darted out the front of the casino and caught a taxi back to my hotel.

I woke up in the morning feeling relatively fresh and pumped for my trip. I sent Calvin a text to see what time they finished up and how he pulled up. He replied to say they kicked on until the early hours of the morning and he pulled up pretty good. He also told me to have a great time on my trip. What a champion. I texted Luke my flight number and arrival time and caught a taxi to the airport. Boarding flights with a hangover was now a thing of the past. I was in a good frame of mind as I checked in. The flight was smooth and once I landed I had a message from Luke to tell me to wait out the front of the airport and to be ready to jump in when he drove by. Like clockwork, I was waiting and ready to go and as soon as I heard the car horn I threw my luggage in the back and jumped into the front passenger seat. Tullamarine Airport is often busy at the best of times, but Luke had planned ahead, and it was a quick pick-up if I do say so myself. Once Luke had navigated out of the busy airport it was good to relax and catch up with another old friend.

Seventeen

Footy Fever

It was going on five years since our trip to the US together and four years since Luke made the move interstate to Geelong. He had also started a family. His partner, Joy, was from the Philippines, and they had a newborn named Jack. We had plenty to catch up on as we chatted on the drive to Geelong. It was dark, so I couldn't really do much sightseeing on the way, though Luke did point out Barwon Prison, but all I could see were some bright lights in the distance. We picked up a carton of beer, but that goes without saying. Joy had heard heaps about me and was very welcoming. They had a cosy and comfortable place with a nice bed set up for me in the lounge room. Once I had settled in, Luke and I went out to his shed for a few beers. The chilly Victorian weather always hit pretty hard, and I was shivering a bit.

I had planned to stay with Luke for the first few days of my trip and over the coming days while he was at work, I would walk to the bus station not far from his place and catch the bus into the main part of Geelong to explore. Geelong is situated right on Corio Bay, which suited me and my fascination with harbours just fine.

During one of the days, I walked out along a pier and found a nice restaurant for lunch overlooking the water. I was back in travelling mode, though this time I didn't need a passport as I was really appreciating what Australia had to offer. Around mid-arvo I would catch the bus back to Luke's place to meet up with him when he finished work, where he would then take me for a drive to do some more sightseeing. On one occasion, Joy and Jack joined us, as Luke drove us to the botanical gardens which offered a beautiful view overlooking the bay. It was also a place overly populated with bats. We also drove by the GMHBA Stadium, where Geelong Football Club play their home games.

My last night at Luke's we all went out for dinner at a local pub where Luke and Joy often went out to eat. I was catching the train the next day into the city where I was booked into a hotel for the next five days including the weekend. Joy's Mum was over from the Philippines staying with them at the time, so Luke and Joy planned to head into the city to catch up with me again over the weekend while Joy's Mum watched Jack. They booked a room at the same hotel I was staying at, and Luke also purchased tickets online for the Eagles versus Saints game at Marvel Stadium on Saturday night. Luke is a fan of the Eagles, while I go for the Saints so what a game to attend! I was boosting!

The next morning, Joy dropped me off at Geelong station and I caught the train into the city. I had a familiar feeling to when I caught the train into the big smoke after spending time with Dad's mate Rob in Aurora during my visit in 2013. I was staying at Batman on Collins which was right across the street from Southern Cross Station. Perfect location! I was well and truly a seasoned traveller now.

After checking in it was time to start planning catch ups with friends in the city. Chipper was the first. Surprisingly, we had only just met at Calvin's 40th. He and his partner met Calvin and Shelley on a Contiki tour years earlier and they all stayed great friends. Chipper was based in Victoria, but he and his partner had flown over to Perth to attend Calvin's 40th. We got chatting at the 40th and seeing as we were both great friends with Calvin, we also connected. Once I found out he was flying back to Victoria a few days later, I got proactive and the next thing, he and I were catching up for a few beers on his lunchbreak at a pub in Docklands on a chilly Friday in Melbourne. I took a pic of us both which I sent to Shelley to let Calvin know we were still celebrating his 40th. According to Shelley he had a big laugh at that one!

Sam was another friend I met at a Guns N' Roses concert in Perth roughly eight years earlier. We kept in touch and seeing as he was now also based in Victoria, he was keen to catch up. Sam used to dive for a living and a few of this old diving crew were currently in Melbourne so he had planned to meet up with them at a pub that night in the Docklands area. He invited me along. New people, new experience, so I was keen. They were all great guys and welcomed me as Sam's friend. I had never been deep sea diving in my life so whenever their conversations about diving got a bit technical, I would just change the subject to football and who won the big game. Lol. I certainly met some different characters, and it ended up being a great Friday night out in Melbourne.

Saturday was going to be another action-packed day. I had been in touch with Shaban and seeing as he was heading into the city to attend the Carlton game at the MCG, we planned to meet at the Crown Casino for lunch. Shaban is always lively company, so it was great to catch up for a beer and plenty of laughs. Even just having lunch is a pleasurable experience when you are in the company of someone like Shaban. Never a dull moment. Afterwards, Shaban headed off to the MCG for the Carlton game while I enjoyed a leisurely stroll over the bridge that spans the Yarra River, back to my hotel.

By this stage Luke and Joy had arrived and checked in so at the designated time, we met downstairs in the lobby for a quiet beer before heading to the game. My excitement started to build while walking through Docklands towards the stadium, in amongst all the other eager supporters. The atmosphere at Marvel was electric. Unfortunately for me, the Eagles won. After a few beers at the game, Luke and I went out for a few more while Joy went back to the hotel. Luke took us to a pub he often frequented whenever he was in the city. As he was spending time with a friend he hadn't seen for a while, Joy had given Luke free reign to have as many beers as he wanted and make a real night of it! This was another classic example of how far I had come with my binge drinking, because after one or two beers at the pub and

Joel Whitwell

just on midnight, it was me who suggested to Luke we finish up and call it a night! The next day was going to be the last time we would see each other for a while so I wanted to be fresh to enjoy one last day in the city with him. While having breakfast in the morning Luke admitted he was surprised but a bit relieved by my decision to have an early night. As a good friend, he was willing to kick on and have a big night with me for "old time's sake". It seems we had both come a long way since we were boosting it up in the US five years earlier. Luke was now a family man, and I had also matured in my own way.

While I was in the city I also contacted Ben. I hadn't met Ben personally yet, but about a year earlier, while I was still feeling a bit lost, a friend of mine felt I needed a mentor to steer me in the right direction, so he put me in contact with Ben. He was based in Victoria and every Monday night he would run Zoom meetings where he would touch on setting goals and breaking old habits to strive to become the best version of ourselves. Naturally, I took a lot out of these meetings and joined in every Monday that I could. Ben knew I did a bit of public speaking so he would engage more and more with me each time to help increase my confidence. That tactic was certainly working. His wife Sharon also joined in on the Zoom meetings and she was lovely and very engaging during the sessions.

Ben told me if I was ever in Melbourne, it would be great to meet in person. So here I was! Ben sent me a message to let me know he was currently renovating a house in Geelong, and if I was happy to meet him there. I pretty much said to Luke, "Looks like I'm coming back to Geelong with you when you go home today." He liked that idea as it meant we would spend a bit more time together before we went our separate ways, for who knows how long! So, once again, I made the trek back to Geelong with Luke and he dropped me off at the address Ben had told me, and I said goodbye to Luke.

It was great to finally meet Ben in person. He seemed a bit quieter than when he was hosting the Zoom meetings, but friendly, and I enjoyed my time in his company. After taking me to one of his favourite pubs for a quick bet, we drove back into the city where we popped by his home in Essendon. He had a lovely place as he took me on a quick tour of his house. I didn't get a chance to meet Sharon as she was out, but I'm sure we will meet on a future visit. Ben then dropped me off at the train station where I caught the train back to Southern Cross Station and my hotel.

I was excited and looking forward to heading up to Hepburn Springs and spending a few days catching up with my old friend from home, Caliopi. I sent Caliopi a message to see if she was still happy to pick me up from the train station in Ballan as originally planned. She replied to say she will be there for sure and if it was okay with me, she was also going to bring her pet pup Jack along to meet me at the station. Bloody oath it was! She didn't even have to ask! I couldn't wait to meet the little guy. So, I caught the train from Southern Cross Station mid-morning for the journey to Ballan.

Eighteen

SCALING MOUNT FRANKLIN

All was going to plan as we arrived at the town of Bacchus Marsh, which was a regular stop. I did start to panic after 15 minutes had gone by and we were still sitting at the station. Finally, the train conductor announced over the loudspeaker that, due to having to do repairs to either the train or track (can't remember which one), we can't go any further and Bacchus Marsh would be the final destination. I started to stress, not for my own situation, as I was now a confident traveller and this was only a minor hiccup, but I thought of Caliopi waiting to pick me up in Ballan and I didn't want to put her out.

I had to act quick so I found a bus that would take me to Ballan and as soon as we pulled out of the terminal, I sent Caliopi a message to let her know of the situation and I may be a bit late. Quick as a flash, she replied, "Cool Beans. I'll just take Jack for a walk while I wait." I slumped back into my seat and had a bit of a chuckle. "How awesome is Caliopi?" I thought. I should never have doubted her. While I can sometimes be a stress-head and get worked up in my mind over minor inconveniences, Caliopi on the other hand, is the opposite. The world could be falling apart around her, and she would just breeze through with the attitude of "She'll be right mate". Nothing seems to faze her, and her easy-going outlook is one of her many great traits. Another good friendship I felt blessed to have in life.

Roughly four years had passed since we last caught up at the Harvey Pub. While Caliopi was travelling the world working as a chef on the boats, I always looked forward to our catch ups down at the local pub whenever she was back home for the summer. We would relax in the beer garden and listen to the birds chirping in the distance while chatting about life and our latest travel experiences. I always enjoyed those carefree summer days down at the pub with Caliopi.

The bus finally dropped me off at Ballan and I was standing in front of the station for less than a minute when I noticed the familiar figure of my old friend coming down the street towards me, being pulled along by an excited Jack Russell which I took to be Jack. After a warm embrace she introduced me to Jack. On the drive to Hepburn Springs, we chatted like old friends do and caught up on what had been happening in our lives since we last saw one another. These days, Caliopi was happily settled in Hepburn Springs and ran her own restaurant "Frank and Connie's" which, by all accounts, was very successful. Her brother Darcy also lived in Hepburn Springs with his family, plus her partner Cara(different Cara) as well as many other friends, so she seemed to have created a good life for herself, which I was happy to hear.

Caliopi lived in one of the two units behind her restaurant, and she had set the spare one up for me to stay during my visit. Once we arrived in Daylesford, Caliopi took me for a tour to show me around her neck of the woods. I couldn't believe how beautiful and scenic Daylesford was. Worthy of a postcard.

A sign from the great beyond. Was that you PJ? Sydney Harbour will always be a special place to create even more memories.

Aberystwyth. A hidden gem I discovered on the coast of Wales.

Beautiful family photo with my niece Jaycee Jean.

Book launch at Harvey Primary School. Another special moment in my life.

Catching up with Tonia in Sydney during the East Coast trip in 2019. Sydney Harbour bridge is lit up for Vivid Sydney. Such a wonderful night.

Dinner wih Sa in Dubbo. The fact that we came together to form a friendship during the height of the pandemic is a testament to the power of human connection.

Doing a bit of reflecting as I often do in life.

'Dreamers can never be tamed. Give peace a chance Belfast'
Signing the Belfast Peace Wall

Emily with the Tarantula. As relaxed as ever. I was comfortable standing over here taking the pic.

Experiencing a spectacular sunset with the lads in Aberystwyth. Another special travel memory.

Hanging out with an English Rose. With Emily in Stratford.

Just passing through the Blue Mountains on my way home from working in Dubbo in 2020.

Kelly's Cellar in Belfast. Ireland. 2018.

Out for dinner in Margaret River with my friends Fiona and Christo to celebrate the book release.

Postcard of Caliopi.

Promoting my book through the magic of photography.

Shakespeare's house in Stratford. A bit of history there. Stratford Upon Avon. 2018.

Shooting clays with the lads on Pat's farm.
Holding the gun like a professional already.

Signing Coralee's copy of my book. Always enjoy our catch ups

Tapping into the positive energy to share my story with the world!!
Doing a photography session with Michael in 2020. Not a pandemic in sight.

The famous Macquarie River. I spent a lot of time wandering along its banks just soul searching. An iconic place in my story.

Visiting the cliffs of Moher.

With Caliopi in Dalysford. East Coast trip. 2019.

With my good friends Dave and Shaun at Shaun's wedding in 2019. The other two scrubbed up well. Me....LOL. Another enjoyable wedding I've attended over the years.

With Katie who included an introduction for this book.

With my good friend Calvin and his wife Shelley celebrating his 40th at Ascot in 2019. One of the most humble and courageous people I have the privilege of knowing.

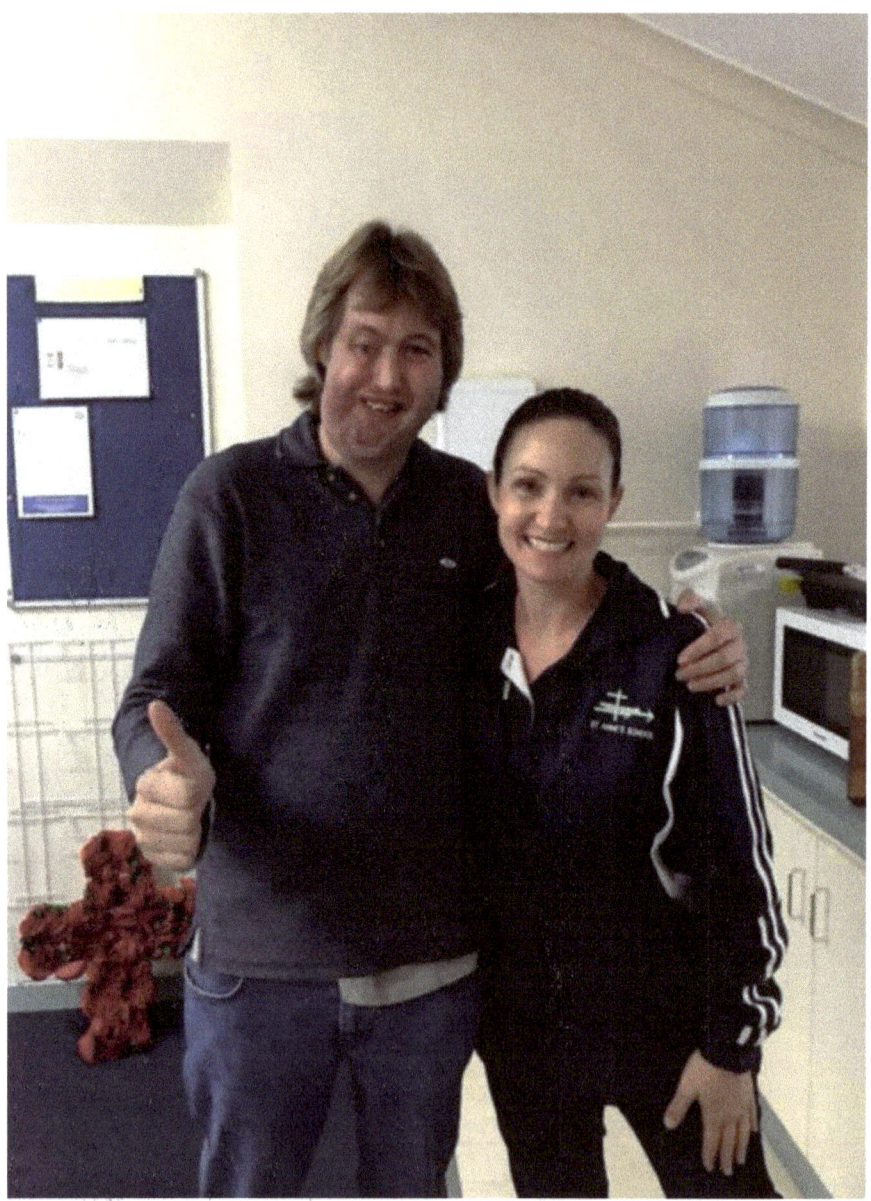

With my good friend Coralee after my speech at St Annes in 2018. I was honoured to have her help with the editing for this book. Such a lovely person and life long friend.

With Rabbie and Ash at my 40th in 2019. Ash has been a good friend over many years. He knows me as well as anyone.

With Shaban at Crown Melbourne in 2019. I always enjoy my time in his company. Legend of a bloke.

With Wongy in front of Parliament House while visiting him in Canberra in 2020. It was great spending time with my old friend.

Daylesford is in the foothills of the Great Dividing Range and all the wildlife was impressive. Caliopi would be pointing things out to me while I was bouncing around in the passenger seat with my phone camera in hand, taking pics here, there and everywhere! It was a very picturesque place. I felt it suited Caliopi's nature, and I was happy to see my friend had found her niche in life. We parked near a scenic lake on the edge of the town to take Jack for another walk. The wind was a bit chilly, but it was nothing compared to the cold wind coming off the water at Ushuaia Harbour during my visit to South America five years earlier, so I handled it okay. Caliopi had her trusted scarf on so she was prepared for the weather. After a nice stroll with Jack around the lake, we headed on to Hepburn Springs and Caliopi's restaurant.

After dropping my stuff off at the unit I was staying in, we both looked at one another with that glint in our eyes. It was time for a beer! Caliopi took me to the local pub in town where we relaxed for a few quiet beers. The conversation and beers flowed naturally. Caliopi still wanted to take me for a drive up to a lookout with beautiful views overlooking the town and surrounding areas, so we only had a couple of beers. We then purchased a takeaway carton of beer to drink at the unit later and made the journey up to the lookout. Caliopi was right. The views were impressive. I imagined Daylesford and Hepburn Springs to be featured on many postcards all over the world. We then headed back to the unit for a few more drinks. Caliopi had a pool table set up in the spare unit so we settled in for a few games and beers. We chatted about our latest travel adventures. Caliopi has a Greek background on her mum's side so if I ever decide to visit Greece on my travels, I know which friend I would ask for advice on its culture and lifestyle. Once she finished work, Cara came to pick us up and the three of us went for dinner at another local pub in town. All up, it was an enjoyable first evening in Hepburn Springs.

I rose early the next morning to the sound of birds chirping and it took me back to the memories of those summer evenings down at the Harvey pub with Caliopi. Seeing as this was my only full day in Hepburn Springs, Caliopi had a big day planned and at the designated time she met me at my unit, and we headed out. First stop was a field just out of town, so Jack could have a run around. Then Caliopi suggested we go for a hike up Mount Franklin. I took a nervous gulp and wandered how big Mount Franklin was. I was suddenly glad we had finished drinking relatively early the night before. Could I somehow talk Caliopi out of it by faking an injury? But she was already heading towards the car with a spring in her step, so I guess we were about to hike up Mount Franklin. Yippee! As we pulled up, I remember looking up at the mountain and thinking "that doesn't look too hard". But as Caliopi soon pointed out, I was looking up at the wrong mountain as Mount Franklin was situated behind us. I thought, "Ok. Now that looks a bit harder." "Let's go," Caliopi said as she started bounding up the side of the mountain with Jack eagerly running alongside her. "Oh well. Here we go," I thought as I picked up a stick to help balance and guide me on the hike.

Less than a quarter of the way up I was already out of breath and really struggling. I looked up at Caliopi further up the mountain who seemed to be doing it easy and wondered, "Where does she get her energy from?" I willed myself to keep going so I did one step at a time. "Nothing beats this traveller," I told myself. This was certainly a test of endurance. I discarded the stick and was now walking up the mountain with my hands on my knees. I was really struggling. Suddenly I heard Caliopi call out, "You can do it Joel. Just think of that nice cold beer we will have later." I looked up to see Caliopi had made it to the top and was standing there with a big smile on her face. She wasn't even out of breath! It seemed like it was just a walk in the park for her. I was out of breath and wanted to give up, but I willed myself to push forward and keep going. I was practically crawling by this stage, but the thought of a cold beer later kind of gave me a second wind. So, I pushed on with all the determination I could muster. By this stage Caliopi was happily playing fetch with Jack while waiting for me to make my way up to the top. I shook my head in disbelief and wondered how she made it up there so easily?

Eventually, after what felt like an eternity, I finally made it to the top where I rolled over onto my back and waited for my breath to come back while looking up at the sky. Though it had almost killed me, I had scaled Mount Franklin! You beauty! This felt a bit different to when I reached the summit of Machu Picchu during my travels through South America five years earlier. On that trip, I took the easy way up by train and bus. There were certainly no trains or buses around to help me reach the top of Mount Franklin. Only the encouragement of Caliopi. "You can do it," and I did.

Caliopi suggested it was almost time for that beer, and in a flash, she and Jack disappeared over the side of the mountain on their way back down. I still hadn't even caught my breath, but I smiled and wondered, "Where would I be without my friends?" Surely heading back down would be a lot easier than heading up I thought. Once I had gotten my breath back I was off bounding down the mountain. Halfway down I noticed a clearing with a spectacular view, so I decided to test Caliopi's endurance by calling out to her to take a picture of me in front of the clearing. Caliopi knows how much I enjoy taking photos wherever I travel so without hesitation she came back up and took the pic. Afterwards, we went for a beer and afternoon tea at the Lavandula Swiss Italian Farm where Cara was working part-time. I really savoured that beer as I took in all the beautiful scenery around me. That evening, I went out for dinner with Caliopi, Cara and a few of their friends. It was another enjoyable evening with plenty of good cheer. Early the next morning, Caliopi sent me a message to see if I wanted to come while she took Jack for a walk before taking me to the train station. Bloody oath I was! While walking along in the crisp morning air I mentioned to Caliopi how surreal it felt that I would be in Sydney that evening. From rural country Victoria to the hustle and bustle of Sydney city! From one extreme to another! From birds chirping in the distance to the sound of noisy traffic. I feel that is the true essence of travelling. Start the day by going for a nice quiet walk in the country and finish it by going out for dinner at a busy restaurant in the city! The time then came for Caliopi to drive me to the Ballan train station and another goodbye was imminent. I had shared so many good times and memories with Caliopi over the years. She was also the friend I chose to reach out to during that weekend at Niagara Falls, where I missed out on the chance of catching up with Marcia five years earlier. So, to spend these last few days with her in Hepburn Springs creating more special memories was awesome.

Nineteen

Cheers to PJ

At the station Caliopi and I had one last big hug goodbye then I boarded the train to continue my journey to Sydney. From Southern Cross Station I caught the shuttle bus out to the airport where I was up and away bound for the Harbour City! I was staying at a nice hotel in Wynard which was only a short walk from the harbour and The Rocks. After checking in I found a busy restaurant for dinner a few blocks from my hotel. Back in my room I sent a few messages to some friends in Sydney to let them know I had arrived safely and to hopefully catch up while I was in town.

James, who I met on that Top Deck tour of Spain back in 2017, replied pretty much straight away to say that he was based in Wollongong but he had to head into the city Friday morning so we could meet up at a café near the town hall at a suitable time. That sounded good to me, so we settled on 11am. I was sure I would also hear from the others over the coming days to plan more catch ups.

I rose in the morning with an excited feeling as I knew I was about to head back to the harbour where I was sure it would bring back those memories from when I visited with PJ on that mystery flight 20 years earlier. I really felt his presence during my last visit for Rhino's wedding nine years earlier. I enjoyed the short stroll to the harbour where all the familiar sights started coming into view – the bridge, Sydney Opera House. All the sights and sounds of the harbour coming to life as I got closer just as it had for PJ and me 20 years before.

I've been lucky enough to have visited harbours in cities all over the world, but visiting Sydney Harbour always gives me a feeling I can't quite describe. There are so many places to eat at Circular Quay, so I had fish and chips for lunch and just took it all in. Afterwards, I ordered a Southern Comfort for old times' sake and sat at a table near the water with an awesome view of the harbour bridge. As a toast to PJ, I put the Southern Comfort on the table and took a photo with the bridge in the background.

The beauty of phone cameras is you can check the photo straight away which I did. I felt a shudder go through me as I looked at the photo. There was a very visible beam of light coming straight down from the sky onto the table right next to the Southern Comfort. I looked all around me, but no beam of light was to be seen! It was only visible in the photo. I figured it must have something to do with my phone, but I had already taken plenty of photos and this had never happened before. It begun to dawn on me that this could only be a sign from the great beyond – that PJ was still watching over me on my travels. "Thanks for the check-in mate," I whispered as I took another sip of the Southern Comfort.

Ever since I can remember, I have always believed there is something greater waiting for us when it is our time to leave this world. I often refer to this as "The Great Beyond". Due to Nanna's faith, I grew up as a Christian and regularly went to church with her. As I got older, I have read up and researched other religions and most notably Buddhism, as the thought of reincarnation strikes a chord with me. But as I sat there that day at Sydney Harbour dwelling on this subject, I still wasn't entirely convinced by any religious teachings. As I go further along in my life's journey, I'm sure I'll continue to research and settle on a faith that makes sense for me. For now, I'm just happy in the belief that there is something greater out there beyond this world we will all experience one day. I'm comfortable with that. I also believe that if you continue to nurture the best parts of yourself, have empathy for others, spread kindness and compassion and do good in the world, then everything should turn out alright wherever you end up. I stand by that belief.

I had almost finished my Southern Comfort when I suddenly realised I had gotten lost in my own thoughts, which wasn't such a bad thing. I wondered what I could do to spend my first full evening in Sydney seeing as I didn't have any catch ups planned until the following day, Friday. As a kid growing up in the West, King's Cross in Sydney was renowned and certainly had a reputation as a place to experience if you ever made it to Sydney. I had driven through it with Mick and PJ on my first visit and my second glance was when Louisa picked me up from the airport when I visited to attend Rhino's wedding back in 2010. Was it now time to take the next step and experience it properly without just driving through?

I decided it was time, so I caught a taxi from Circular Quay to the notorious King's Cross. On the way, the taxi driver told me that it had been cleaned up recently, but things could still happen there so, his words to me were, "Just be careful". I gulped and wondered what I was getting myself into, seeing as I was on my own. But the urge to at least check it out was just too strong. Besides, there was still a few hours of daylight, so I told myself if I didn't feel comfortable I could just head back to the safety of my hotel before nightfall. What could possibly go wrong at the Cross? I shuddered at the thought.

The taxi driver finally dropped me off as I took in my surroundings. I guess they were right when they said the shire council had taken steps to clean it up because at first glance there didn't appear to be anything out of place in this wacky place I had heard so much about. No drag queens getting around or crackheads stumbling about – not yet anyway! It just looked like perfectly normal citizens going about their everyday lives. I decided to do what I normally do whenever I experience a new place, so I found a pub for a few drinks to ponder my next move. For some reason I decided to go against my normal routine of drinking mid-strength and ordered a Southern Comfort, seeing as the first one I had down by the harbour went down nicely. If alarm bells weren't going off in my head, they soon would be.

I was halfway through my drink when I received a message from Tonia to inform me that even though she had a busy schedule over the coming days, she was hoping to catch up at some stage while I was in Sydney. She lives in Hornsby which was quite a way out of the city so to be already planning on heading in to catch up with me despite her busy schedule showed the type of person she was. I thought back to the memories from when we first met each other during our Top Deck tour through Spain a few years earlier and with any luck we would be catching up again right here in Sydney soon. I was sure she would work something out as I took another sip of my drink. I was in a fairly relaxed mood when I suddenly heard a noise outside, so I peered out the window to see what it was. I saw a man standing there having an animated conversation with himself. He was speaking in third person, having a good old chinwag. He then suddenly started hooting like an owl. "Owls are nocturnal creatures and only come out at night," I thought to myself. I was intrigued, but also nervous by this spectacle. He was either mentally unstable or my first glimpse of a true crackhead. He then started going on a huge rant and marching around. Wow! He was putting on a bit of a show for me and I had free entry! "Can someone pass the popcorn please?" Lol. But on a serious note, I did feel sympathetic towards his plight as no one should be out in the community in that frame of mind. Suddenly, he was now a ballerina! I must admit, he danced well and had some decent moves! I had come into King's Cross expecting to see something unusual and out of the ordinary, but I was starting to think I had gotten more than I bargained for here.

After a while, I lost interest and went back to pondering life over a few more drinks. I was halfway through my fourth Southern Comfort when alarm bells started going off in my head. I felt very relaxed and had a nice buzz going on. I knew this feeling well. It was time to drink up, let loose and have a big night out in King's Cross no matter the consequences! For old times' sake, one bender surely wouldn't hurt? Seeing as Southern Comfort is a lot stronger than mid-strength beer, without really thinking about it, I knew I had now put myself in a precarious position.

Twenty

OH CANADA!

I had to think quick as it was starting to get dark outside. I was tempted to roll the dice one more time, right here in The Cross and have a drunken night out which could be reckless considering how far I had come over the last few years. I had crossed the line into temptation and there was no turning back. Suddenly a light bulb moment occurred in my mind. Seeing as I have been single my whole life and had never been in a relationship, every once in a while I like to indulge in a bit of passion with a prostitute, especially when I travel. Amsterdam comes to mind!! I have plenty of female friends in my life as I connect well with them, I really enjoy their company. But for some reason I had never been able to take the next step beyond friendship. I feel blessed to have all these female friendships, but we all want to have a bit of passion in life sometimes, right? Temptation was calling me away from the Cross which was the plan. So, I looked up a few profiles on my phone and found a Canadian prostitute not far from my hotel, perfect. I got in touch with her, and we arranged a time for me to arrive at her place for a bit of passion, just as the Southern Comforts were going down too well and I needed to leave King's Cross and the temptations lurking there. Saved by the bell, I hailed a taxi and left the temptations of The Cross behind in the rear-view mirror.

I have always had a thing for Canadians and their sweet nature, so I was looking forward to this Canadian encounter! She lived in a nice area with the harbour bridge visible in the distance gleaming in the moonlight. At the designated time I knocked on her door and as soon as she opened it my good eye almost popped out of my head and I'm pretty sure my glass eye did! She was gorgeous and yes, she was Canadian all the way from Vancouver! Oh Canada! She invited me in and I found her very easy to talk to, like all Canadians I have met on my travels. We got lost in conversation before we remembered what I was there for! So, she led me into the bedroom for some sweet Canadian passion and she certainly didn't disappoint! Wow! Best money I ever spent! Oh Canada! I was walking on air when I left her apartment so using the harbour bridge as a guide, I decided to walk back to my hotel. I was in a happy mood as I started singing the lyrics to the nursery rhyme "London Bridge is falling down, falling down, falling down. My fair lady." I must have still been feeling the effects of the Southern Comforts I had earlier as for a moment there, I forgot what city I was in! All this travelling I had done was really messing with my head. Haha. Not long after I arrived back to my room, I received a text from "Oh Canada" to thank me for being such a gentleman while in her company. This was a first for me, as I had never received a thank you text from a prostitute before! She was very attractive, friendly, had confident vibes, intelligent and a goddess in the bedroom. It got me thinking and I wondered what attracts some people to become prostitutes when they could easily have other paths they could have taken in life? Was it the allure of fast money that could help give them a lavish lifestyle? Either way, I certainly wasn't complaining as I was sure I would be seeing "Oh Canada" again on this trip!

Twenty-One

Time to Catch Up

After having a bit of fun experiencing more of what Sydney had to offer, it was now time to start catching up with friends so on Friday morning I walked to town hall for my catch up with James. It was good seeing him again, two years on from our Top Deck tour. James gets a bit excited and as a local he felt obliged to come up with suggestions to help me get the most out of my time in NSW. Go to an NRL game, check out Newcastle and Wollongong, go see the Blue Mountains, go hiking through the forest – the list went on. I was only here for a few more days, but I must admit, I couldn't help but get caught up in his enthusiasm. Like me, he seemed like a real go-getter.

Back at my hotel I received a message from Louisa. She is one of my oldest childhood friends from growing up in Myalup who has now called Sydney home for the last 30 years or so. As I wrote in the first book, I always planned to stay with her and her husband Adrian when I was visiting Sydney. Seeing as it was Friday and I had no other catch ups planned for that day, we decided that night would be perfect for me to stay. They lived out in Western Sydney, so she planned to pick me up from Redfern Station after she finished work around 5pm. I caught the subway out to meet Louisa and it was great to see her again as we chatted just like old friends do, on the drive back to her place.

Louisa and Adrian had recently purchased a two-storey house in a nice neighbourhood in the outer suburbs of West Sydney. The house was a credit to how hard both had worked over the years. They had now secured their dream home. It appeared to be a comfortable lifestyle, and I was happy for them both. The perfect environment to raise their two children, both boys.

Once Adrian arrived home from work, he cooked up a feed on the barbeque. Afterwards, the three of us enjoyed a few beers in the spacious carport. Unlike the last drinking session, we had together while I was staying with them in Ryde nine years earlier, I was able to remember this one.

On the way to the subway in the morning, Louisa first took me around to her Mum Pam's place so I could also catch up with her while I was there. She then dropped me off at the station so I could make my way back into the city.

Back in the city I wondered what I could do for the rest of the day, and I decided it was time to catch a ferry out to Manly since I had heard so many great things about it. I wanted to see for myself what all the hype was about. I boarded the ferry on that beautiful sunny Saturday in Sydney and took in the spectacular scene of the harbour as we pulled away from Circular Quay. Stepping off the ferry and walking along the boardwalk through the centre of Manly was spectacular. I had a positive vibe about the place as I stopped to watch a busker play some beautiful melodies. At the end of the boardwalk was the ocean which really soothed my soul. I was so happy I had finally taken the time to check out the magical scenery Manly had to offer. It was bliss. While I was out there, I received a message from Tonia to see if I was free Monday evening as she could head into the city for a catch up then. If I wasn't free, I certainly was now because I was really looking forward to catching up with her again, especially since we had connected so well on the Top Deck tour two years earlier. Also, seeing as I was flying out for Brisbane on Tuesday what a special finish to my time in Sydney that would be. So, it was all set.

I also heard from Aaron, and I planned to meet up with him and his partner Rachel for breakfast at Circular Quay in the morning. I first met Aaron and Rachel on that Contiki tour I did with Luke through the US which I wrote about in my first book. Hopefully they don't bring up my big night out in Vegas, but I was sure they would. Lol. Just on dusk I caught the ferry back to finish another great day.

In the morning, I met up with Aaron and Rachel at a café on Circular Quay. After their mock wedding in Vegas, they had since had a proper wedding and were now married for real. It was great to see them again as we reminisced about good times on Contiki and yes, at some point, my big night out in Vegas did come up as a topic of conversation. I was starting to wonder if I would ever be able to live that night down. Haha.

After breakfast and a nice catch-up I decided to head to The Orient for a Sunday "sesh" seeing as the day was still young. I had heard the Sunday sesh at The Orient usually went off and I was certainly in the mood for some beer and live music. It was time to head back to the very place where PJ and I had met up with his Uncle Mick on that mystery flight all those years ago.

The Orient really sticks out and is clearly visible. I discovered if you stand at a certain spot in the harbour you can see it nestled away in the distance inviting travellers like myself to come in for a drink or two. I felt obliged to do just that whenever I visited Sydney as I always found the welcoming atmosphere refreshing. This Sunday was no different, and after enjoying a few beers I got chatting to some of the locals and was having a great time. The live band started to play, and the atmosphere went up a notch. Even better, they were playing classic Aussie rock anthems. This was what I would call a true Sunday sesh right in the heart of Sydney. The Orient was rocking, and I was right amongst it. I was having such a fun time that for a minute there I felt like I was rocking it out in heaven. I raised my glass and whispered "Cheers" as a tribute to PJ. Unfortunately, I was having too much of a good time because after a while the alarm bells started going off in my head again. I was sticking to mid-strength beers which was a good thing, but I found they were starting to go down way too fast for my liking. Things were starting to become a little hazy. On reflection of my life, I have found that whenever I get caught up in the moment, it would often lead to drinking too much and blacking out. It was certainly a pattern in my youth and now that I was once again caught up in the moment, I needed to heed the warnings and make a responsible decision. It was time to do the White Ninja and disappear from that environment before I had too many beers. But seeing as the night was still young and I had a buzz on, I needed something exciting to do to keep the night going a bit longer before heading back to my hotel. I won't give too much away in this book, but I will give you a clue as to how the rest of my night went. Oh Canada!!!

Twenty-Two

Vivid Sydney

The following day was my last full day in Sydney and seeing as I had plans to catch up with Tonia that night I decided to rest up and take it easy. I was excited to see her again and I wanted to make it a memorable night for both of us. We planned to meet up out the front of my hotel around 7pm. Just on nightfall I got ready and around 7pm I headed down to wait for Tonia out the front. From where I was standing, I had a clear view of the subway from where Tonia would be arriving. I must have been deep in thought as I didn't see her exit the subway and it wasn't until I looked to my right and noticed someone walking towards me with their arms waving in the air to get my attention. Tonia had arrived.

After a warm embrace we wondered what we could do to make the most of our time together, Tonia knew some good places to eat so she suggested we go for dinner while I suggested we go for a night stroll around the harbour. We decided to do both. Tonia knew of a popular restaurant located not far from the harbour which had pizza on the menu, so we settled on that. Who doesn't love a good pizza? Just like that last night in San Sebastian, we had a great chat as we walked towards the harbour, picking up where we left off in Spain. It was already shaping up to be a wonderful evening.

We found the restaurant and settled in for a lovely meal. As expected, we both ordered pizzas to share along with a beer each. While we chatted, Tonia told me that after graduating from Sydney university not long before our Spanish trip, she had gone on to secure a working role at the university as a speech pathologist. It was nice to hear that, as it sounded like she was really enjoying still being involved with the Uni in some capacity. The conversation continued to flow as we enjoyed the pizza and beer, just happy to be in the moment and each other's company.

After dinner we went for a nice stroll around the harbour. As luck would have it, we were there when they were setting up for "Vivid Sydney" which is an annual celebration of creativity, innovation and technology. Throughout the event colourful and bright lights illuminate the city, in mainly purple hues. It was awe-inspiring to witness at night, and I felt blessed to share that with Tonia. And to add to the occasion, Tonia was wearing a purple top, which made it even better! No planning on her part, just a wonderful coincidence.

Once we reached the Sydney Opera House we took a few photos of one another on the steps of the forecourt, just as I had with PJ 20 years earlier. Wow! Twenty years ago. I had a sense that wherever he was in the great beyond he knew I was back. The purple lights of the city and bridge reflected off the water as we went for a walk around the Opera House.

After a few hours Tonia needed to catch the subway back to Hornsby, so we started to head back towards my hotel. It was such a magical night and one of those moments you wish would never end. I couldn't have asked for a better finish to my time in Sydney. Tonia decided to catch the subway at Circular Quay, so we said our goodbyes and parted ways. I thought about the moment we had just shared and how lucky I was to have met someone like Tonia. She was such a genuine and caring person. I guess choosing to sit in the empty seat next to Tonia at dinner that night we first met has proved to be a great decision on my part.

Once back in my room I sent Tonia a message to see that she made it back to Hornsby safely. She replied to thank me for a wonderful evening. It was now time to focus on Queensland and the last stage of my journey.

Twenty-Three

Heading Back to The Lads

One of the lads, Lachy Evans, was currently based in Brisbane and was going to pick me up from the airport. Pat had also set up a messaging group so we could all keep in touch for the duration of my time in Queensland. He also informed me of what he had planned for my visit. A few of the lads were going to meet up with me that weekend on the Gold Coast for a night out. After that I would be heading back with them to Toowoomba where I would be staying with Cowie in Aubigny for a few days. This would be followed by a few days at Pat's parents place where he lived when he wasn't travelling the world with work. He also informed me to be prepared for a bit of clay shooting and beer drinking! Wow! I had never done clay shooting before, so I was excited to hear that. The beer drinking on the other hand…haha, don't think I need to prepare for that as I've had plenty of practice! It was certainly shaping up to be an epic finish to my trip.

I had also heard from Bec, who is a good friend of my cousin Lauren, to let me know she will be on holiday at the Gold Coast with her ex-partner Richie and their kids while I was there, and if I wanted to catch up. I was keen as I also knew Richie from growing up in Harvey. Even though they were separated, I thought it was nice they were keeping it civil by going on holiday with the kids. It showed a bit of character. I was catching up with friends here, there and everywhere on this trip.

The flight to sunny Queensland was a smooth one and true to his word, Lachy was waiting for me out the front of the airport. Champion. We chatted as we drove into Brisbane in his yellow Mitsubishi Lancer. Lachy was telling me about his travels back to Europe earlier in the year and I discovered he was a lot like me with his love of travel, making memories and having that feeling of nostalgia – a kindred spirit in the making.

I was staying at the Great Southern Hotel, which was located right in the heart of the city. Lachy dropped me off and we planned to catch up again for a drink over the coming days when he finished work. I spent the following days exploring Brisbane on foot. I went for a stroll through the botanic gardens and along the Brisbane River. Even though it was sunny when I arrived there was now a slight drizzle. I felt my senses start to heighten as I let all the memories come flooding back, including memories of that day in Venice. I always seem to go back to that day in Venice in my quieter moments. Maybe it was that Contiki tour in all its entirety that has stayed with me all these years?

After a few days of reflecting, it was time to catch up with Lachy for a few drinks. He was currently going through a fitness phase, so he stuck to water while I happily had a few beers as all the walking I had undertaken the previous days had worked up a thirst! Besides, the number of times I would bend my elbow to bring a nice cold beer to my lips is a form of exercise! Lol. After catching up with Lachy I went for dinner at an Irish pub not far from my hotel. It brought back memories from my travels through Ireland the previous year.

On Friday morning it was time to start my journey to the Gold Coast. Wow, how exciting! Like in Ireland I was certainly leaving no stone unturned in my quest for new and exciting experiences in my life. One thing was for sure, I wasn't going to die wondering. To travel is to really push the limits and gives more depth to one's life. I felt proud of how far I had come since that first overseas trip to Canada with Dad way back in 2004. While on the train I thought back to my visit to the Cliffs of Moher, which reminded me of another travel quote I like. "May the road rise up to meet you. May the wind always be at your back."

I had also been in touch with another friend, Grant, who I knew from back home in my younger years. He was currently based on the Gold Coast, and we were also planning on catching up once I arrived. The last time we caught up was at Rhino's wedding in Sydney nine years earlier, so it had been a while between drinks! We planned to meet at the Hard Rock in Surfer's Paradise when I arrived. As soon as I stepped off the platform at the train station I was immediately taken aback by all the high-rise buildings surrounding me. Even though I wasn't a surfer, it still felt like paradise. I found the Hard Rock Café and settled in with a beer to wait for Grant. He arrived not long after and it was good seeing him again after all this time. We spoke of the night at Rhino's wedding when I didn't have any accommodation booked so in my drunken state I was going around asking everyone if they had any spare room for me to stay. Grant was one of the people I asked, but unfortunately it was full where he was staying. He asked how the rest of my night panned out and I told him how I latched on to our mutual friend Atho and his partner and wouldn't let them out of my sight as that seemed to be my only hope for somewhere to stay. On the other hand, seeing as they had just attended a wedding, Atho's partner wanted some romantic alone time with him, so she wasn't too keen on having a drunken friend cramping their style. They tried in vain to lose me, but I was very persistent, and we all know how the story ended. Haha. Grant had a big laugh at that. I told him I included that story in my first book, *One Eye. One Ear. No Worries,* and he said he couldn't wait to read it one day.

Grant had a free afternoon so after a few beers he walked with me to my hotel. We planned to meet up again at my hotel in the morning so Grant could show me around. I seemed to go well having friends as tour guides wherever I travel.

That night Richie and Bec picked me up from my hotel as we headed out for dinner and a night on the town. After an awesome feed we hit up the Broadbeach Casino for a fun night. Richie kept trying his luck on the roulette wheel and two-up. From memory he lost more than he won though he was never without a glass of bourbon in his hand. What a champion. Bec had the kids so left at a reasonable time, but Richie and I kicked on and had a pretty big night! He would tell me later that night was the best of the trip!

Twenty-Four

Old Habits Do Die Hard

Grant met me at my hotel in the morning and we spent a great day checking out Surfer's Paradise, just the tonic I needed after a big one the night before. We went for a walk to the beach before Grant showed me a few of the many canals that run through the city. Once again, my thoughts drifted back to Venice and Amsterdam. We then went up to Sky Point Observation Deck which offered impressive views of the city.

After a good day with Grant, by late afternoon it was almost time for my next catch-up. Pat had booked a suite at the Hilton as he and a few of the lads were currently on their way into the city for a boosting night. With all the fun I had with the lads on my travels through Ireland and Wales the previous year, I couldn't wait to see them again. A reunion on the Gold Coast! I couldn't have scripted it any better. At a designated time, I met Pat and the others in the lobby. He was with Dan and Dougal. Lachy was currently on his way from Brisbane. Due to work commitments, Cowie couldn't make it, but I was planning on staying with him for a night or two when I travelled to Toowoomba later with the other lads.

We headed up to our suite and I must say, Pat had really outdone himself! It was like a bachelor pad and the balcony offered spectacular views overlooking Surfer's Paradise. I thought back to the movie *The Hangover* and my big night out in Vegas five years earlier. I wondered what kind of mischief we were about to get up to. Could this be a repeat performance? No. I had come too far to go back to old habits now. I convinced myself I was going to keep my drinking in check. I could set a good example for the lads, who were a bit younger than me. Maybe even influence them to become more responsible drinkers perhaps?

Colbey was another friend from back in the days growing up in Harvey, as he used to hang out with PJ and me and our group of mates. He left town not long after PJ's passing and was now settled on the Gold Coast. He also wanted to catch up while I was there, so I invited him up to our suite for a few beers and to meet the lads. With Lachy also arriving, we all sat out on the balcony, knocking back the beers and catching up high above the bright lights of the Gold Coast. Due to my binge drinking past, I was being a bit of a mentor, encouraging the others to pace themselves and drink steady as the night was still young. As a seasoned binge drinker who had come out the other side recently, I was proud of myself for keeping the others in check – or trying to!

We then went for dinner and ended up at a night club just down from our hotel. Suddenly Pat appeared with a tray of mixed drinks and shots. Seeing as I had been well behaved up until then I figured one wouldn't hurt, for old time's sake…or would it? The next thing I remember was waking up in bed. The sun was up so I figured it was the morning. Once I started to regain my bearings, I felt relieved to find I made it back to the suite, but then to my horror, I discovered I wasn't in my own bed. I was in Pat's bed! He even had all his stuff in there, but lucky for me he wasn't in the bed! I was alone. I breathed a sigh of relief as I remembered waking up in bed next to Dumma in Scotland 10 years earlier. Even though Pat was a great guy I certainly didn't want to go through that again! Lol.

I walked into the other room to find Pat sitting there. He started laughing as I sat down. I sheepishly asked him what happened? He said he went to go to bed last night to find me already passed out in his bed. I was sleeping like a baby so, being the gentleman that he is, he didn't want to disturb me and decided to just go and sleep in my bed. In other words, we swapped beds for the night. Man, I thought I was passed all that! Old habits do die hard.

When the others woke up we soon found out that Dan had slept on the bathroom floor while Dougal had thrown up all over the Hilton's nice carpet. We certainly had a big night for my reunion with the lads and I still had a few more days to get through. Hopefully the finish to my trip doesn't get too crazy, I thought, as it hadn't had the most promising start. Haha.

After a good breakfast to settle the hangovers, it was time to leave the bright lights of Surfer's Paradise for Toowoomba. Dougal and Lachy had a wedding to attend so they had left earlier while I travelled with Pat and Dan. It was an enjoyable trip which offered me the chance to see more of outback Queensland.

Twenty-Five

CRUISING ALONG THE DUSTY ROADS IN THE VOLVO

As we hit the outskirts of Toowoomba Pat pointed out Tabletop Mountain in the distance. It was impressive, Dan also kept pointing out other scenic views from the back seat, so I had to keep craning my neck to look. Once we arrived, we dropped Dan off, then Pat took me on a tour through the town. Toowoomba was a lot bigger than I thought it was. Plenty of pubs, which was in stark contrast to the one pub we have back home in Harvey! We then drove out of town to Aubigny where Pat and Cowie were both from. Aubigny was a lot like Wokalup with only a pub and a few houses. Maybe a general store, but I didn't see one on that trip. Pat and Cowie had both talked up the legendary Aubigny Pub so I wondered if it would match The Woky. I was sure I would soon find out. Lol.

Pat took me to Cowie's lettuce farm which he was now running after taking over from his Dad and keeping it in the family. He was hard at work when we arrived but gave me a big embrace and finished up for the day, so we were soon having beers. Cowie was living in a house on the farm, and if I remember correctly, I'm pretty sure it was the family house where he grew up. After visiting Pat's parents where I would soon be staying for a few nights, we met up with the other lads for a night on the town. We were all well behaved except for Cowie. He must have gotten a bit excited by my presence as he ended up passing out in one of the bars and was soon evicted. Legend. Including our night on the Gold Coast, five of us had now had a drunken misadventure in the past 24 hours. They all definitely reminded me of my younger years. Always up for a good time whenever possible. Maybe it was destiny that I was able to meet such kindred spirits as myself.

I spent the following days mainly in the passenger seat of Cowie's Volvo as he showed me all around Aubigny. To be honest, there wasn't much to see, but I enjoyed the experience, nonetheless, cruising along the dusty roads in the Volvo. This was country living at its best and as a country boy myself, I felt right at home, especially with all the dust coming up from the wheels. Cruising the back roads of Aubigny in the Volvo, or was it the main roads? Lol.

Seeing as it was a hot and dusty day, I finally got to experience the Aubigny pub as Cowie took me there for a midday beer. The Volvo was sitting right out the front of the pub which would have made a fitting postcard – I'm sure that would have boosted tourism in Aubigny! There were three older gentlemen sitting at the bar as we walked in and of course Cowie knew one of them. They got chatting and I took him to be either his Pop or a good friend of his dad's. That's the thing about country pubs; there's a good chance you'll bump into someone you know. I looked around to see it anyone recognised me, but I was a long way from home, so it was highly unlikely. I also visited the pub on another night with Pat and Cowie. I was certainly receiving the whole Aubigny experience on this trip as I was leaving no dusty stones unturned in my thirst for adventure.

After a few days, Cowie dropped me off at Pat's parents place where I would be staying for the remainder of my duration at Aubigny. They had a nice house on quite a few acres of land and were very welcoming as I settled in. Pat then gave me a tour of the property. Now for the thrilling part of the trip – Pat asked if I had ever done clay shooting before? I told him that being from WA, I hadn't. He then went to the shed and pulled out the pulley machine that launches the clay targets along with a gun, and his dad joined us for a bit of target practice. They were very cautious and took the time to show me how to use the gun in a safe manner.

Boy, was I excited and eager to start blasting some clays, but I decided to stand back and let the experts go first. With his dad manning the pulley machine Pat would say "Pull" which was the signal to launch the clay target. Pat would then take aim and casually blast the clay target in half. Between him and his dad, they hardly missed! They made it look easy. When it was my turn, they helped me with the gun so I could handle it properly. I then yelled "Pull" as Pat launched the clay target. I took aim with my good eye and fired. Wow! The force of the blast almost knocked me off my feet, but I regained my composure as I watched the fully intact clay target disappear into the horizon. Not the best start. I don't think I hit any clays that day, but I enjoyed the experience all the same.

Seeing as I was due to head back to Brisbane on the Sunday, Pat's parents hosted a gathering at their place on the Saturday as Pat invited the other lads around for a few drinks and a catch-up before I left. They also put on an awesome feed. I thought that was nice of Pat's parents to do that for me, but that's the type of people they were. Delicious food, awesome company, cold beers flowing and a bit of clay shooting! All the ingredients for an enjoyable day.

After a few beers I decided to give the clay shooting another go. Unlike the previous time I felt quite relaxed as I casually took aim with my good eye, fired and blasted the clay target in half! I turned to Pat with a grin and asked him to grab me another beer. I ended up hitting a few clays and had three helpings of food washed down with plenty of beer. Pat and his parents had really gone the extra mile by hosting that gathering, and I will always appreciate everything they did for me on that trip. It was a fitting finish to my time in Aubigny as no one was accidentally hit by a stray bullet and I can now add "professional clay shooter" to my growing list of expertise. Lol.

The next day I took in the serenity of Aubigny one last time as Pat drove me to Dougal's place in Toowoomba and from there I was going to grab a lift with Lachy as he drove back to Brisbane. I had grown fond of the lads, so having to say goodbye to them again was tough. Even though I still had a few days left in Brisbane my mind was already starting to turn towards another journey home. On the drive back to Brisbane, as we did when he had first picked me up from the airport, Lachy and I had a great chat. The conversation just flowed. As a young man, it sounded like he already knew what he wanted out of life, in particular travelling and making memories. Sound familiar? It was dark when we arrived back in Brisbane, so Lachy took me on a detour up to a lookout that offered great views of Brisbane at night. I was certainly spoilt as people kept going out of their way to help me get the most out of my trip right to the end. I had booked my last few nights back at the Great Southern Hotel, and as Lachy dropped me off we planned to meet up for one last drink before I left.

And then, just like that, I was on my own again. I spent my last few days just resting up and going for a few strolls through the city with my thoughts. I met up with Lachy for that drink at a pub not far from the Gabba. Finally, it was time to head to the airport for home. As I always do when I travel on the flight back to WA, I thought about the trip I had been on and what I had got out of it. After heaps of overseas travel, it was nice to get the chance of seeing more of Australia. We live in a beautiful country with heaps of scenic landscape to explore.

Another thing that really meant a lot was every single person I had originally planned to catch up with on this trip made the effort and caught up with me. I know people are busy in their own lives, but it all fell together nicely as one after another I was able to catch up with friends as I made my way along the east coast. That gave me a special feeling in my heart to know I can connect with people on a personal level whether I was with country lads or city folk. I had felt just as comfortable going for a walk under the bright lights of Sydney with Tonia as I did shooting clays on Pat's farm. I believe anyone who comes into your life has something to share, and I found that out more than ever on this trip. A gift, if you will.

Twenty-Six

FREE AS A BIRD

While on that flight home I also thought about all the other friendships I have been lucky enough to have made in my life. Shaun Goodman was one of those friendships that came to mind. I first met Shaun through Davey near the end of 2009. Those two had grown up together and had always been close friends. Davey had told Shaun a lot about me and vice versa so I guess it was only a matter of time before we met and also became friends. Davey lived in Lake Clifton, so it was only natural I met Shaun on a night out at the Lake Clifton Tavern with Davey. We hit it off straight away. Shaun had got married earlier that year in 2019 with Davey as his best man and me a guest at the wedding. By this stage I had lost count of the weddings I had been to over the years, but they are always great fun and seem to be the only time I dance these days.

I was reminiscing about Shaun's wedding as the plane came into land, but not before I thought of another friend, Ben 'Chooky' Upton. We had also grown up together and I would also attend his wedding in the future. I chuckled to myself as I suddenly remembered something he did once after a few too many beers which I received a few looks from the other passengers in my direction. 'Oops!!' Another trip done and dusted as I touched back down on WA soil. It was back to work and reality once again. By this point in time,

I had now been working for the government as a meat inspector for six years and even though I have had opportunities to secure a permanent position with the department, I hadn't applied due to the fact I enjoyed the freedom of travelling around and filling in at different meatworks as a casual. Even though it may come back to bite me down the track, as being permanent meant security, the lifestyle of travelling around as a casual suited me at that time.

I have always been a free bird with my travelling, so I didn't want to get tied down too much. Plus, I was very reliable, so my boss looked after me and made sure I had plenty of work. He rang me one day to ask if I was interested in filling in as the fourth inspector at Katanning Meatworks over the summer. Seeing as I was a casual employee, all my accommodation would be paid for as well as a travel allowance to drive back home for the weekends. Oh, the perks of having a government job! I didn't want to let him down, so I told him I was keen. Even though it didn't sound like Katanning had much to offer in terms of excitement, I was determined to make this another positive experience for me.

Before my stint in Katanning, I was also required to fill in for a week in Narrogin. So, it was back to the Albert Facey Hotel. For anyone who doesn't know the story of Albert Facey, he wrote a book near the end of his life titled *A Fortunate Life* which would go on to become a bestseller and inspire heaps of plays based on his life story. My connection to Albert is that Normie, who is my best friend from school, is his great grandson. So, it was surreal I was staying in a hotel named after him!

Not long before I was due to leave for my stint in Narrogin, Tom Marlow, who was a reporter for Channel 7, must have heard about my story and reached out to see if I was interested in doing a segment on my life. How awesome was that! Bloody oath I was! So, we planned to meet up at Koombana Bay in Bunbury for an interview. The universe seemed to be rewarding me for keeping a positive outlook as I was about to make my television debut sharing my story with the world. This was sure to reach many more people. Boy, was I excited!

On the designated day, I met up with Tom and his cameraman at Koombana Bay which proved to be a very scenic backdrop for the interview.

He asked if I could bring along with me the handwritten pages of the first book I was writing which would eventually become *One Eye. One Ear. No Worries. A Story of Resilience*. Doing the interview and in front of the camera I felt like I naturally belonged, so I believed now more than ever it was my destiny to share my story as a source of inspiration for others. Tom got some good footage of me strolling along Koombana Bay deep in thought and reading through my handwritten autobiography. I believe he did a good job capturing the essence of my story and I couldn't wait to see how it came across on the small screen.

A few days later I packed my things and headed off to Narrogin for a week. Once I finished work on the Monday, I saw I had received a message from Tom to let me know they would be broadcasting my story on the news that evening. Wow! That was quick. Instead of going back to my accommodation, I decided to head straight to the pub where I would watch it there. So, I walked in, checked with the publican if the TV was on the right channel, ordered a meal and took a seat in the restaurant area with a clear view of the TV and bar area.

A few of the locals were sitting at the bar and once my story came on they were fixated on the TV. About halfway through I noticed one of them took his eyes away from the TV to have a quick glance over at the restaurant area. He and I made eye contact. He continued to look around and suddenly he glanced back at me then looked back at the TV. I knew straight away what he was thinking. The inspirational man he was currently watching on TV was sitting right there in person in the restaurant area. How often does that happen? Circumstances like that are very rare.

After watching me on TV he and his mates came up to shake my hand and buy me a beer. Being on TV certainly does have its perks, especially being in a new town! I thought Tom did a wonderful job capturing the essence of my story. The locals in Narrogin certainly thought so too as the week I was there quite a few of the meatworkers came up to shake my hand and congratulate me on the good job I did on TV. It was like a celebrity was in town for a week working as a meat inspector! Great timing Tom!

Courtney was the OPV (On Plant Vet) based at the Narrogin meatworks and, as is often the case with me, I struck up a good relationship with her while I was there. She had seen and done a bit in her life, so I found her easy to talk to. If you are interested in what they have to say I have found most people are easy to chat to, especially over a few beers!

One evening after work we went for dinner together at the local pub. It was the night after my segment on TV, so my spirits were quite high. Courtney had a bubbly personality anyway, so we were both in a happy frame of mind as we toasted one another over my successful television debut. Things were looking up.

Another night Courtney and her friend took me for a drive to show me Dryandra Woodland National Park which wasn't far from Narrogin. Courtney's friend worked at the park as a guide so on that night she took a small group, including Courtney and I on a tour through the park which was lit up with lights as well as the bright stars in the sky above us. It was fascinating to watch the nocturnal creatures such as the bilby, bandicoot and wallaby casually come out to greet us at different spots on the tour. I was now really starting to appreciate all different kinds of experiences on my travels.

Twenty-Seven

ALL THE VETS AND A MEAT INSPECTOR

After I finished work on the Friday, I took the memories of an interesting week with me as I left Narrogin and headed home for the weekend. It was time to set my mind to a stint in Katanning as the fourth meat inspector over the summer. Katanning is a small Wheatbelt town nestled in the heart of the Great Southern of Western Australia with a population of 3500 thousand people. To be honest, there wasn't much to do there in terms of excitement as I had discovered during my previous stints working there, but like every other time in my life, I was determined to make the most of the experience I had in front of me. Plus, I had already told my boss I would do it, so I couldn't let him down!

From growing up in a small town and being a country boy myself I was confident I would be able to fit in with all the locals in another small town. As I started packing my things for the drive to Katanning, little did I know how much of an impression I was going to make there. Lol. My boss had booked me into the New Lodge Motel which was located just off the main drag as you turn into town. As I checked in and was walking to my room, I couldn't believe it as I heard someone call out "Hey Whitty". Turned out it was Wayne Johnston, with whom I had worked at Harvey Beef 20 years earlier! These days he was living down in Albany and working on the roadworks. He was now working in a different industry but was based in Katanning for work over the summer. Staying at the same hotel as well! What were the odds? Seeing as there were two pubs in town, I knew we would be having a few beers together during our time in Katanning too!

I continued walking to my room shaking my head in bewilderment as my ability to bump into people I know, no matter how far or wide I roam, was uncanny! As I was soon to find out, I also knew the Q.A(Quality Assurance) manager who was based at Katanning Meatworks, as I had also worked with him at Harvey Beef previously. His name was Marc, and we would regularly catch up for a beer outside of work hours. And of course, I knew the other inspectors that worked there. Already knowing a few people in town helped me settle in well. After a few drinking sessions at both pubs, I was starting to feel like a local already.

The two pubs in town were the Feddy and Exchange, and I found out the Feddy had skimpies every Thursday. I thought Kalgoorlie was the only place that had skimpies these days. I figured Thursday to be my main drinking night while I was in town! I wasn't in town too long when I heard there was a third bar you can drink at. Somehow, I always seem to find these things out. Lol. The Cordial Bar was pretty much hidden in the basement of the Dome. Yes, Katanning had a Dome in town! It used to be the Old Premier Mill which had closed years earlier. After sitting as an abandoned building for ages it was decided to transform the old mill into a Dome with hotel rooms on the upper floors for tourists and locals to enjoy a coffee and stay overnight. Wow!! Pretty much a five-star hotel and Dome right in the heart of Katanning.

I quickly became a regular for my after-work coffee, then, if I was in the mood, I would nip down into the basement for a quiet beer at the Cordial Bar. Even though it was quite dark and still had a bit of a basement feel, it had plenty of different beers to sample and was often frequented by many interesting characters to chat with. Every small town has them, and I was quick to make myself at home. Often during that summer of 2019-20 you would find me perched at the Cordial Bar enjoying a cold beverage after a long hot day at work.

Due to my position as a meat inspector, I had the privilege of already knowing a few of the local veterinarians in the area. Jenni was the vet based out at Beaufort River Meatworks. Every Thursday I would catch up with them at the Dome for a social catch up. We were also joined by Jim who had been the vet at Katanning Meatworks for years before recently retiring. No wonder, as he was in his 80s but he had a good stint. An older couple who ran their own vet practice from home just on the outskirts of town also often joined us. All these vets and a meat inspector. I was in elite company.

After my Thursday catch ups with the vets at the Dome I would often wander over to the Feddy where I would meet up with Wayne and some of his workmates for a drinking session – served by the skimpies with their tits hanging out. Marc also sometimes joined us. I was really coming into my own that summer in Katanning as someone who felt confident and comfortable in the company of people from all walks of life. I felt just at home chatting to the vets about animals, politics and history as I did relaxing at the bar with Wayne, Marc and all the boys while copping an eyeful of the skimpies boobs! I found I could fit in anywhere.

While working in Katanning that summer I felt something starting to come back that I have often struggled with at different stages in my life. Loneliness is something we can all relate to on certain levels. As I wrote in my first book, it all came to a head and almost engulfed me while staying on a boat in Stockholm Harbour back in 2016. Like then, I was again away from home, this time for work purposes. Even though I'm a very connected and sociable person who seems to make friends wherever I go, the loneliness often lingers below the surface. Even though I was doing everything right while in Katanning regarding staying connected and catching up with people, I was spending the nights back in my hotel room alone with my thoughts.

As I had while sitting in my car at Myalup Beach after PJ passed all those years earlier, I found I was thinking deeply about life while spending those long nights alone in my hotel room. At that stage in my life of having recently turned 40, I had never been in a relationship, and that was playing on my mind a bit. Everywhere I looked, people seemed to be staying or jumping in and out of relationships, and yet it still hadn't happened for me. It dawned on me that I have been single and gone to bed alone every night of my life. How I longed to have a partner I could cuddle and just chat about life while listening to the rain or wind howling outside. By this stage I had trained my mind to see the positives in everything. So, instead of feeling pity for myself, I thought, "Wow, I am actually a strong person."

Twenty-Eight

Going Down the Rabbit Hole

There is a bit of power that comes with learning to be alone. And look at the life I have created for myself? An extraordinary life full of travel. Not to mention all the special memories I had shared with people along the way. Plus, I have so many female friendships in my life, and I will continue to nurture them. I have also come to believe that patience is a virtue so while I'm waiting for my soul mate and I to cross paths, I'll just keep putting myself out there, meeting people and living my best life. I feel whoever I end up with as a life partner will be the luckiest lady on earth to have such a patient and kind-hearted person to share life with.

My heart will never accept the reason I have been single all this time is because of being born the way I was, as I believe it is better to have loved and lost than to have never loved at all. Doesn't everyone deserve to find love at least once in their life? I'll just keep spreading my message that beauty comes from within, and I know more and more people will continue to gravitate towards me because of the light I radiate. With all the travelling I do I could cross paths with my soulmate anywhere in the world. It could be a place such as London, Paris or New York. How exciting – something worth waiting for.

In saying that, I am blessed to have so many good friends I could reach out to whenever I was feeling a bit lonely, and Ash was one of those friends as we were in regular contact during my stint in Katanning. Being a friend over so many years he knows me as well as anyone, and I remember him telling me while chatting over the phone one night to not go too far down the rabbit hole or I could get lost in my thoughts. He knows me well, and I'll always appreciate him being there whenever I've needed a friend to talk to.

I also thought about my friendship with Anastasia. After a few years of keeping in regular contact she suddenly stopped replying to my messages. After a couple of messages with no reply I decided to let it go and move on, but I often wondered what I did wrong as we seemed to be getting along well. One night while I was in Katanning I saw that she posted a picture of her wedding on Facebook. It all made sense now as I decided to try see things from her perspective. She had obviously met someone and once things started to become serious between them she figured it wouldn't be fair to her partner if she stayed in touch with her friend from Australia. Well, that's what I believed.

A part of me was happy for her, but another part was sad as I enjoyed the friendship and hearing all about her latest travel adventures. I felt that was a bit of a shame as like all the other females in my life we were just friends, and I was no threat to her husband. Plus, I honestly believe my story was going to impact the world one day and I wanted Anastasia to be a part of that on a friendship level. Oh well, her loss. I just hope her marriage lasts and she found her happily ever after. Either way, I'm pretty sure she will hear more about my life one day.

Memories I made on Contiki '09 stayed with me more than any other memory I made in my life, but I now had mixed feelings about that trip. Along with Marcia, I now had two friendships I had made on that trip come to an end. Whether it was a friendship or another great trip I often struggled when they came to an end. Sometimes I feel I am too sensitive for this world, but as long as I have a purpose and a reason to live, I'll find it in my heart to keep going.

Around this time something exciting was starting to happen in my life. Someone who knew I was making good progress with my autobiography put me in contact with her friend Fleur who was an editor. Not long before my stint in Katanning, I met up with Fleur for a coffee at Dome in Bunbury. After hearing more about my autobiography, she was keen to work with me on this project. That was a very good call, as it would go a long way towards making my dream of publishing my first book a reality. She must have seen something. So, I gave her the two handwritten completed books. I was confident what I had written was in good hands. Little did we know that first meeting at the Dome would be the start of another friendship.

Every month or so while I was in Katanning, Fleur would email me the edited version of my autobiography, section by section. I would always look forward to going back over what I had written. Seeing as it was *my* story, Fleur didn't change or tinker with it too much. Mainly a tidy-up job with a touch of female perspective. She also put it into chapters and came up with all the titles for each chapter. She deserves credit for the wonderful job she did with my first book *One Eye. One Ear. No Worries*.

During those long, lonely summer nights in Katanning, I also thought back to an experience I had in the town when I was a teenager. As I mentioned in my first book, I used to compete for the local fire brigade during my mid-teens with my brothers and a great group of mates. Dad was the coach and Mum used to help out too, so it was pretty much a family affair. On the weekends we would all catch the fire brigade bus to participate in demonstrations in different towns throughout the state.

One weekend, we had a demonstration in Katanning, so we all planned to stay overnight. They booked us into an old-style building which was until recently abandoned before the council decided to turn it into a hostel. It had a creepy feel about it, and my imagination ran wild which led me to believe it may be haunted. My first experience of Katanning.

That evening we all went to the local speedway for a night out. Troy and Calvin were two friends from the fire brigade who were with me that night as we walked into the speedway. I noticed two young local girls giggling and chatting to one another while pointing in my direction as we entered the complex. Suddenly, one of them quickly came up to me while her friend was trying to pull her back. Without hesitation, she pointed to her friend and said she wanted to go on a date with me. Her friend quickly put a hand over her mouth and dragged her away. They both almost fell over in hysterics. For them it was probably just a bit of harmless teenage fun, but for me, it broke my heart. My disfigurement had become the object of their little joke, and it hurt. I didn't tell Troy and Calvin what happened as I didn't want to put a downer on what was shaping up to be a fun night out in Katanning.

As teenagers we had discovered something that would become one of my big loves throughout my adult life – beer. After the speedway, we got one of the older guys to purchase some for us. We finished the night laughing and stumbling through the streets of Katanning towards a big light in the distance which we were hoping was our haunted hostel. Thankfully it was.

While lying in bed thinking about that night and the memory all these years later, I wondered how I was able to turn that night around into an enjoyable memory? From starting the night with a harrowing experience to finishing it laughing and having fun with my friends? I wondered if we were born with resilience, or does it develop through our struggles and hardships in life? Did I already have resilience in me that night at the speedway as a teenager? Let's be honest here, beer always has a knack of turning most teenage experiences into a fun time. Haha. But even then, I was already showing signs of resilience, and instead of withdrawing more into myself away from people and life whenever I encountered a negative experience, I kept a positive outlook.

I never did see those girls again. For my own peace of mind, I let it go straight away and didn't have any ill feelings or animosity towards them. I just hope that as they grew into adults, they found empathy and became more aware of other people's feelings.

Twenty-Nine

Taking Control of My Own Destiny

As someone who often read the newspaper and watched the news, I was in tune with events happening in the world. I remember while on my way home from Katanning one weekend early in the new year, reading an article about a virus that had recently found its origins in Wuhan. It was called Coronavirus and seemed to be spreading throughout China. Seeing as it was happening overseas in China, I wasn't too concerned or interested when I first read about it, but as I and the rest of the world would soon find out, it was going to impact us way more than we could ever imagine!

Whatever is happening in China will hopefully stay in China, I remembered thinking. So, for now, it was back to Katanning for another week of work. Besides, we are worlds away from China, so what could possibly happen in Katanning I thought? I was surprised to stumble across a makeshift nightclub in town while heading back to my hotel the night after attending the Katanning Show, so I was confident that no matter what happened out there in the world there wouldn't be a ripple effect big enough to reach Katanning. I thought Harvey was sheltered in a bubble, but shit, Katanning is something else. I still can't believe that for one night after the show every year there is a nightclub in town, let alone a deadly virus that came from China running rampant throughout the town. I chuckled at the thought.

Early in the year I decided to get proactive and see if I could get my story out there around the Great Southern seeing as it wasn't my local area. Kind of like what I did in Narrogin. So, I looked up the local journalist in Katanning and went for a walk to see him about doing something with my story while I was in town. From the front it looked to be a derelict old house which I took to be the journo's office. But to my dismay, when I knocked it appeared to be empty and deserted. "Good old Katanning," I thought. "What chance do I have for sharing my story here?" I was just about to concede defeat when I noticed the sign on the door advising they were now based at an office in Albany. It had an email address for Liam Croy so I figured it wouldn't hurt to at least reach out to him and see what happened.

Liam was one of the local journalists in Albany. I wasn't expecting much so I was quite surprised when I received a call from him not long after to say he loved my story and could certainly do something with it. I was elated to hear that. The TED talk I did back in 2017 really helped a lot as it seemed to attract people's interest. Liam asked if I was happy to do the interview in Albany or Katanning? I figured Katanning could do with a bit of exposure and a boost for tourism in the town, so we settled on meeting there. The Dome and the centre of town would make a scenic backdrop for my story. It was all set.

The following Sunday I left home earlier to meet up with Liam in Katanning for the interview. We sat in the foyer of the Dome where we conducted the interview followed by taking a few pics of me out the front. For someone who wasn't even a local, I'm sure the town appreciated what I did that day to give it more exposure to the outside world. My story was to be included in the *Great Southern Herald* which meant my story was now spreading throughout the Great Southern region of the State. I had created something positive all because I had been sent to a remote area with work and was able to get proactive. Even better, I made the front page with a great photo too. Underneath the headline read, "Heart and Soul" which was quite fitting, I thought.

Maybe the spirits of the Inca and Peruvian people were watching over me as I felt something profound was starting to happen in my life. The message that had germinated in me during my travels throughout Peru was now maturing via my journey – from the wonders of Peru all the way to Katanning. What a journey! Lol. Liam also posted the interview online which was well received. Like Narrogin, once the newspaper came out with my story, I was immediately recognisable as I went about my day in Katanning. Now that the locals had more of an understanding of the background of my story, I was met with warm greetings wherever I went. Not that I needed any help, as I felt I had already done a pretty good job mingling with the locals and making a name for myself even before the story came out. I was starting to learn that we can control our own destiny, or at least have a say in the outcome of our lives.

Thirty

The Virus Strikes

In February, I received an invite to attend my old friend Newby's buck's party in March. He was planning a weekend getaway with the boys in Melbourne for late March. Unlike some of my other close friends who had moved away, Newby and I drifted apart a bit once he left Harvey, but we had shared some good memories together and I still remembered him fondly. It had now been almost eight years since Flemo's wedding in Canada when Newby and I spent the weekend at Niagara Falls, so that memory always comes to mind pretty quickly. Plus, Adam was going to be there, and I knew plenty of the others who would be going, so I figured it would be a great reunion and catch up with everyone. Knowing Newby, it was going to be an epic couple of days. I was keen to be a part of it for sure. I was rubbing my hands together with glee thinking of the antics we would all get up to!

Throughout it all in the early months of 2020, I kept hearing media and news reports focusing on the Coronavirus and how it was affecting heaps of people in China. It seemed to be spreading rapidly but it was happening there, not here, so nothing to worry about. I couldn't work out why the media was so caught up in it all? Suddenly it was being reported that people were dying from it! Still, China is a very long way away.

Wayne had two new people working with him on his crew, Nigel and Wade, who I also got to know through my friendship with Wayne. The three of us spent a bit of time together as we were all staying in the same hotel. I was also getting excited for Newby's buck's party weekend in Melbourne which was coming up quickly. I was watching the news in my hotel room one evening when suddenly it was reported that Coronavirus had been detected in someone from outside of China. Then another, then another, then another. "Interesting!" I thought as I sipped my beer. But still, it wasn't here in Australia, so hopefully still nothing to worry about. It then seemed to be spreading throughout the US and parts of Europe. The media were becoming consumed by it as fear and paranoia were spreading quicker than the virus itself! Still, I figured Katanning was too isolated and rural for a virus spreading throughout the world to impact us here.

Finally, a few days later, the inevitable happened, as it was detected on the east coast. It had penetrated our borders from overseas and was now in Australia and spreading fast! The media was all over it, so you couldn't really escape the hype, even in Katanning. You would have to be living under a rock if you hadn't heard of the Coronavirus by then. It was closing in fast as it continued to form a dark shadow over the world. Countries were starting to go into lockdown and people were being banished to their homes for protection. I remember watching footage from Milan Italy. Everyone was in their homes when one lonely person wandered out onto his balcony and started singing in a high-pitched voice to try to lift other people's spirits in the uncertain times. Soon everyone else in the vicinity was also on their balconies and singing along. It was a powerful moment, and I was impressed by what I saw. The power of positive thinking.

I wondered if we could show the same fortitude here in Australia. Everyone in Katanning seemed to be on edge as we were now faced with uncertain times. There had been pandemics throughout history before, but none in our time. The Black Death which spread throughout Western Europe, Asia and North Africa in the 1300s resulted in the deaths of 75-100 million people. Surely this latest pandemic was going to be mild compared to that one I thought. The media didn't seem to think so, as it continued its crusade of ramping up the fear and uncertainty. But, like anyone who has a good heart, I value human life, and in these early stages if people, especially older people, were succumbing to this virus then I had to follow the rules to keep people safe and slow the spread. I did have a few doubts though as some things didn't add up. Like when someone contracted or passed away from the virus, the media wouldn't mention the person's name. Instead, they would just tally up numbers. In this age of technology, we have so much information at our fingertips, but I can almost guarantee if you were to Google the name of the first person to contract or succumb to the virus in Australia, you wouldn't be able to find it. I'm not claiming to be an expert, so I could be wrong. Just an observation.

Everything was starting to close and go into lockdown as the virus continued to spread throughout the east coast, and with Newby's buck's party in Melbourne only a week or so away, everyone was anxiously awaiting news on whether it was still going ahead or not. I was invited to a barbecue at Jenni's place on the Sunday before I was due to fly out for the buck's party. It was at this barbecue where I met John Paul who would become a good friend of mine. It was also at this barbecue that a message came through on the group chat to inform us the Melbourne trip was cancelled, and we were now having the buck's party in Perth. Under the circumstances, it was probably the right decision as I didn't want to be known as the person who brought the virus into Katanning from interstate after celebrating a friend's buck's party in Melbourne. It wouldn't go down too well with the locals. Lol.

I had already booked the Friday and Monday off work, so I now had to turn my attention to spending the weekend in Perth instead of Melbourne. No jet setting for me this time. Unless of course someone pulls out a joint and I feel inclined to indulge, but these days I very rarely, if ever, dabble unless I'm in Amsterdam. That scenario was highly unlikely, but I guess you never know! It was a buck's party so anything could happen. Oh yeah, there was also this very deadly virus according to the media that was quickly closing in on WA to consider. Man, I was excited! This was shaping up to be a bigger weekend than I first thought.

I booked my accommodation then set off for Perth from Katanning on the Friday morning. On the drive, every radio station seemed to be fixated on the Coronavirus. You couldn't escape the hype unless you were living under a rock and even then, you would probably still be impacted. Suddenly, the WA premier issued a press release saying WA was going to implement social distancing rules later that day where we had to keep a distance of 1.5 metres from one another. With a ban on huge gatherings already in place, this was shaping up to be a race against time to spend one last weekend with friends for a while before we all went into lockdown which now seemed inevitable.

While on the highway, I noticed a steady stream of traffic going the opposite way in a rush. Like in the movies whenever a major catastrophe happens, everyone wants to leave the cities in a hurry. I, on the other hand, was heading straight into the city and to be honest, I was relishing the excitement I was feeling of the unknown. Kind of like when I first started travelling and not knowing what to expect. This was shaping up to be a buck's party for the ages. I checked into the Great Eastern Motor Lodge once I arrived in the city. I enjoyed a nice cold beer while relaxing in my room and thought about all the insanity happening around me. I didn't know it then, but worse was to come.

The buck's party was to run over two days as we were planning to gather at a pub in the city that night followed by a bus trip to a country pub the next day. After a few beers, I got ready and took the lift down to the lobby. Just before the doors were about to close, a random guy came running up and joined me in the lift. We got chatting and I noticed he had an accent. He then informed me he had flown in from New Zealand the night before. Immediately, alarm bells started going off as I wondered why isn't this guy in quarantine, and moreover, what if he has brought the Coronavirus in from overseas and I was in the process of contracting it from him where I would then spread it everywhere at the buck's party? The lift suddenly seemed very small and I didn't remember a motor lodge having that many floors! I tried to look calm while he, on the other hand, looked like he didn't have a care in the world. He was even cracking jokes though I was having trouble seeing the funny side. I kept thinking please don't cough or sneeze on me or in my general direction. Finally, after what felt like an eternity, the lift doors flew open, and I took off in a flash followed by a cheery "catch ya later" from a potentially disease-ridden lift companion.

While sitting in the taxi on the way to the pub I told myself not to let my paranoia get the better of me in these uncertain times and just enjoy myself at the buck's party. "Oh wait. Was that a mild sniffle I heard from the taxi driver?" I thought. I arrived at the pub with no symptoms to find a few of the crew were already there including Adam. The beers were flowing as well as the conversation. After a while everyone seemed to forget about the big bad virus the media kept going on about as we enjoyed ourselves. Every so often someone would remember and attempt to put 1.5 metres between himself and the person he was drinking with, but a few beers later they would forget again as they were virtually high fiving and hugging the other person. I admit I was probably the culprit of doing that a few times. Lol. True to form, Adam accidentally dropped a couple of pint glasses, so we were all probably enjoying the festivities a bit too much. Coronavirus wouldn't even dare enter the pub and disturb our revelries – or would it? We still had another day to get through, so I called it a night at a reasonable time and fell asleep back at my hotel with no symptoms to speak of, just a mild fuzzy drunk feeling.

The following morning, we all met at the casino to catch the bus for our pub crawl to a country pub. Newby and Adam were running late as Newby had to take his dog to the vet. Hey, he had priorities he had to take care of. Plus, it was his buck's party so, even if we were feeling a bit thirsty, we just had to wait a while. Eventually they turned up and right on cue we boarded the bus just as the Eskys were opened. The destination was Northam, but we stopped at some pubs along the way. It was really my scene. After a lovely afternoon enjoying the four walls of a pub in Northam and seeing nothing else of the town, we slowly made our way back to the city stopping at a few more pubs along the way.

It was dark by the time we arrived back in the city and seeing as it had already been a big day, I decided to make my getaway before things got too messy. Between pubs I noticed we were in the vicinity of my hotel, so

I discreetly planned with the bus driver to drop me off where I bolted back to my accommodation before the temptation to join the others at the next pub got the better of me. To be honest, everyone on the bus was probably too drunk by this stage to notice someone from their group had suddenly vanished. The White Ninja strikes again. I was becoming more accustomed at knowing the right time to leave the party and call it a night before old habits could surface. I guess leaving a buck's party was a pretty good gauge to see where I was at. Social distancing on the other hand… It was certainly a buck's party to remember, and no one showed any symptoms that weren't alcohol related.

I had booked an extra night and wasn't due to head back to Katanning until the Monday, so I spent Sunday just relaxing. After blocking it out as successfully as I could to enjoy the buck's party, news of the Coronavirus started to close in around me again. There really wasn't any way of escaping it. Trust me, I tried. Watching round one of the AFL in my hotel room gave me some respite from the madness, but even then, there was no crowd at the games due to the virus.

On the Monday I checked out and started the long drive back to Katanning. As I drove along Albany Highway I kept listening to the news reports on the radio. Step by step all businesses and cafes were shutting down and closing their doors including restaurants and pubs. Phew! We certainly cut it fine with the buck's party. Suddenly the big announcement came through that WA was shutting its borders to the outside world so no overseas or interstate travellers could enter. It all started to feel even more real now. I pulled over and sat in a park to try get my head around it all.

Everything felt very quiet and eerie that day, like I was caught up in the twilight zone. Maybe it was the twilight zone, and I was the main actor in a new series. No, my imagination was running wild again. This was really happening, so I had to try make sense of it all. Even worse, I was heading back to Katanning which can often have a depressing feel even in normal times! It felt like a dark cloud was forming around me and in my mind. For someone who has inspired people with my positive attitude, this was shaping up to be a test. But in saying that, this was something everyone else in the world was also going through so I was determined to face up and get through it the best I could.

I decided in those early stages, the best way to keep my spirits up was to stay in regular contact with family and friends and not get too isolated even though the government and media seemed to be doing everything in their power to keep us all apart. Maybe it was for the greater cause as we all went into lockdown. Locked down in Katanning. Wow! How do I find myself in these situations?

Seeing as I was a government meat inspector I was classified as an "essential worker" so I had to keep turning up to work which probably wasn't a bad thing as I believe I would have suffered a bad case of cabin fever if I was forced to stay in my hotel room all day every day. Just when I thought I had seen and heard it all, I saw all the stores and supermarkets in the region had sold out of toilet paper! At first, I thought I must have turned on the comedy channel by accident and it was just a joke. But to my horror, I soon realised it was the news and was happening! I always look for the good in people and like to think I can read people well, but in that moment I couldn't understand humanity.

It boggled my mind more than anything else that had happened in my life. And right on cue, footage emerged of people fighting in a supermarket over the last of the toilet paper! All I could do was grab myself a cold beer and settle in to watch the show which I still perceived as comedy. The world as I knew it had become one big circus with clowns and magicians everywhere just making all the toilet paper disappear! Lol. I was beyond bewildered. Just when I thought I had seen it all something else will pop up.

I was lucky to have a good group of friends in Katanning to share the start of this uncertain experience with. We had to social distance so I, together with Wayne, Nigel and another of their workmates, would sit out the front of our rooms drinking and chatting while maintaining a distance of 1.5 metres between us. These were strange times indeed. Then the mask wearing came in, so another rule to follow. I also noticed there was a lot of finger pointing going on with people quick to cast out and make an example of anyone they felt wasn't following the rules. It was madness.

This has been one of the most unfortunate aspects of COVID which the Coronavirus was also known as. The way people dobbed others in or ostracized them if they weren't vaccinated or wearing a mask. Why couldn't we all find a way to stick together and help one another get through these uncertain times? Fear does funny things to people. I thought back to my experience in Amsterdam a few years earlier when I was on magic mushrooms and everyone around me seemed to be alien. The thought of that made me chuckle. It was astonishing I was comparing this new reality we were facing to an experience I had in Amsterdam while high on magic mushrooms!

Thirty-One

Magnum PI

In late March my boss phoned to let me know of an opportunity for some work interstate for a meat inspector in either Dubbo or Singleton and wanted to see if I was interested? It sounded like an amazing opportunity, and I knew I would regret it down the track if I didn't give it a go. But then, I remembered the world had pretty much just gone into lockdown due to a pandemic, and here I was entertaining the possibility of travelling interstate to NSW which was a hot spot for the virus! Was I crazy? Maybe I was, or maybe I just I liked the idea of another adventure.

The way I saw it, being locked down in Dubbo sounded like a way better proposition than being stuck in lockdown in Katanning. Plus, I had discovered over my journey, that whenever I had left my comfort zone, though it appeared daunting at first, it helped me to grow as a person. It's the steps you take that help you discover your full potential in life. I was ready to test myself again. I told him I was keen, and he told me he would book my flight for mid-April and organise a few weeks accommodation. We decided on a couple of weeks to start with, but if I was willing to stay longer, we would just extend it. He said he would also fax through a letter to show the custom officials at the airport letting them know I was required to enter NSW as an essential worker.

Wow! I was starting to feel like Magnum PI. Haha. Here I was about to travel again albeit for work purposes this time. I was excited, but also anxious. I still couldn't get my head around the fact I was about to take the biggest step in my career, and it happened to be right at the start of a worldwide pandemic where everyone was being put into lockdown! I pondered the idea again that I *may be* crazy!

The plan was to fly to Sydney on April 17, catch my connecting flight on to Dubbo, pick up a hire car from the airport, and drive to the meat works to commence work. "Oh, remember to also wear a mask and don't come down with any symptoms," is what I was told. I should be able to manage that. Seeing as no one was allowed to cross regions without a valid excuse, Mum dropped me off at the station in Harvey early that morning in April so I could catch the train to Perth to begin my next big, exciting, but uncertain adventure.

I had been in touch with my old friend Adam, and I was planning on spending the morning at his place before getting dropped off at the airport. After taking my seat I received a nice surprise. Carter, who I knew from boosting up in Harvey back in the day, also happened to be catching the train to Perth. He quickly changed his seat to the spare one beside me as we started chatting about old times and friends we used to know.

Chatting to Carter helped calm down my nerves as we shared a few laughs. Once we disembarked in Perth, I said my goodbyes to Carter and caught a taxi to Adam's place. It was nice spending that morning with my old friend and travel companion on some of my earlier trips. We had both come a long way since drinking at the bars in Thailand 14 years earlier. Along with the friendship we have, he was also a big help in the early stages of my travels. We have shared so many good times and memories over the years, both overseas and at home. Adam called Perth home these days and I got the sense that city life suited him, but like all of us, I feel he never lost that country upbringing. I guess it is instilled in us all.

Thirty-Two

NOT IN KANSAS ANYMORE

I arrived in Sydney that evening and after a few nervous moments waiting for the custom officials to go over the letter from the department stating I was allowed to enter NSW as an essential worker without having to quarantine. I was finally ushered through. You beauty! I certainly wasn't mentally prepared to have to quarantine for two weeks. Plus, I hadn't packed enough books to last for two weeks. I would have gone stir-crazy!

I was booked into a hotel near the airport before I caught a connecting flight to Dubbo first thing in the morning. While walking to my hotel it suddenly dawned on me that I was now smack-bang in the middle of a hotspot for the virus! It made me think of a memorable quote from the classic movie *Wizard of Oz* where Dorothy says, "We aren't in Kansas anymore Toto". I wasn't in fortress WA anymore. The streets around the airport were pretty much deserted due to people being in lockdown. Just a lone Sandgroper making my way to the hotel. The stillness felt eerie. This would be a different memory of the Sydney that I would become used to in the years to come.

After a quiet night, I was back at the airport first thing in the morning to catch my connecting flight to Dubbo. I chuckled at the irony. Even during a pandemic, I still couldn't manage to stay away from airports. Lol.

Country NSW here I come! Boosting! I picked up the hire car from the airport and took off in search of the meatworks. Sightseeing and having a good look around Dubbo would have to wait. I found the vet's office and he led me onto the floor to introduce me to Pat who was the regular meat inspector at the Dubbo meatworks. I found Pat to be a great guy, and we clicked pretty easily which was a relief, as that was sure to make my experience in Dubbo more enjoyable seeing as we were working together.

I got to know him quite well and I discovered he was a fan of Meatloaf and loved playing golf on the weekend. He was about to go on leave so he showed me the ropes of how everything was done for when I would be working with the relief inspectors while he was away. With my experience of working in different meatworks back home in the West, I was confident I could handle it.

After that first day at work, I checked into my accommodation and settled in to start my Dubbo experience. Pat was great that first week while I was finding my feet. It was hard trying to navigate a new place during a pandemic. Ordering dinner at night was often a hassle as almost everything was shut. I quickly got into the routine of ringing up and having takeaway delivered to my room. I certainly get didn't get to see much of Dubbo during my first weeks there, pretty much just the meatworks and my accommodation. Heading into winter I also found it to be colder than I was used to back home.

While Pat was on leave, I was able to hold the fort, and it was nice to get to know some of the relief inspectors who had travelled from different parts of NSW to fill in while Pat was away. The owner of the meatworks lived in a nice house at the top of a hill overlooking the plant which I would get a clear view of whenever I left the meatworks at the end of my shift. You couldn't really miss it, even though there was often fog around on the colder days, especially up in the hills. He was an older guy who had obviously done well in the industry as he also owned a meatworks in Albany as well as Dubbo. Every day like clockwork he would make his way through the plant to check that everything was running smoothly.

Without fail, he would always stop by the inspector's station to have a chat, which I always enjoyed. While I inspected, he often would get excited, and while slapping the side of a carcass would say quite cheerily, "How are these big boys?" which I would find amusing. He was a character. Bob was an old German guy who would trim the carcasses and had plenty of stories to share. I reckon I must have heard all his stories in between inspecting. Haha.

Besides that, I found my first few weeks in Dubbo quite challenging. Not being able to do anything besides going to and from work and my accommodation due to the pandemic was tough, and being away from home didn't help. My routine for those weeks was: I'll drop by the Bottle-O after I finished work on the Friday, grab myself a carton and spend Friday night and Saturday just relaxing at my hotel, having a beer, listening to music and thinking about life in general. I didn't want the drinking on my own to develop into another habit I would have to confront further down the track, but for that little while in Dubbo it felt quite peaceful. Besides, everything was shut down so I couldn't really do much else. Come to think of it even though things eventually opened for me, I pretty much kept the same routine the whole time I was in Dubbo.

Thirty-Three

That Wonderful Afternoon at a Park in Dubbo

Seeing as I had a bit of time on my hands outside of work hours, I decided to learn more about the town. Straight away I discovered it was classed as a city instead of a town. Interesting. Dubbo's name apparently meant "red soil", which was supposedly consistent with the local landscape. I was yet to see much of the red soil during my stay in the city, but I planned to keep on the lookout for it! There had to be some there somewhere!

I learned that Dubbo has the largest population of the Orana region of NSW. It is linked by national highways to all the major cities on the east coast. The Macquarie River runs through the city, and it is also the name given to the main street in Dubbo. Macquarie Street, as I was to discover later in my stay, was dotted with pubs. It also featured the Old Dubbo Gaol, a library and plenty of cafes. Hey, I was getting better at picking out points of interest besides pubs whenever I visited a new place. Lol. Dubbo also lies between the Great Dividing Range to the east and the plains of the Darling Basin to the west. I was sure I would find out more about Dubbo when I visited the Old Dubbo Gaol which I planned to do when everything opened again, whenever that might be.

Due to protocol, after three weeks my boss had to book me into accommodation that provided cooking facilities, so I was on the move again to a different part of Dubbo. I've never been much of a cook, but we had to follow protocol, so after work one day I followed the GPS to my new accommodation. Wow, Dubbo was bigger than I thought. I was happy with the new digs as it had a nice park over the road right on the banks of the Macquarie River. Perfect for walking and soul searching. It also had plenty of fast-food outlets in the area and included a main road that seemed to stretch forever into the horizon as far as the eye could see, no matter what direction you were facing!

Like most of the other meatworks I had been based at, the Dubbo plant also had plenty of overseas backpackers working there. One day I got chatting to a nice lady from France. Her name was Sa. She was half French and half Madagascan. We enjoyed chatting those first few days, so we exchanged contact details and planned to also catch up outside of work hours while we were both in Dubbo. I liked that idea as the isolation I was feeling from being a long way from home during a pandemic was starting to make me feel lonely again. It would be nice having a female companion to spend time with while in Dubbo. I was from WA, she was from France, and we both had to travel to Dubbo for us to meet. It certainly had the makings of another good story.

We planned to meet up the following Sunday at a park not far from her accommodation. As I often do, I arrived a little early to be there for when she arrived. I had some plastic cups and a few beers in a cooler bag so we could each enjoy a quiet beer while we chatted. Soon enough, a taxi pulled up and Sa got out. She had arrived! Seeing her without a mask and in a different attire than her work uniform made my heart flutter a little. She had an aura about her and an elegance that I found very captivating. I poured her a beer into a plastic cup and handed it to her which she graciously accepted. What a special day it was already shaping up to be. It was a massive park which offered views of my old accommodation way off in the distance. Like at work, we seemed to enjoy each other's company as we sipped our beer and chatted on that wonderful afternoon in a Dubbo park.

The weather was overcast and there were plenty of gloomy clouds in the sky, but I was certain that even if it did start raining, it still wouldn't ruin the moment! I enjoyed hearing about her life growing up in France and trips she made to Madagascar – certainly a different upbringing to mine! I also told her a bit about growing up in Harvey, though seeing as we had only just met, I was careful not to go into too much detail about all the reckless and crazy antics that my friends and I got up to! Haha. I figured she would find all that out if she ever read my book *One Eye. One Ear. No Worries*. I had to keep some parts of my life for her to enjoy in the book!

Eventually, we had to call it a day as it was starting to get dark, but that day was the best I had since first arriving in Dubbo. The power of human connection would overcome any pandemic that was doing its best to keep people apart. Sa and I coming together to create a friendship during a pandemic is a testament to that. I certainly had a warm feeling in my heart once I arrived back at my accommodation that night. Seeing as the rule seemed to be changing all the time, I wondered if we were supposed to wear masks during our catch up? Oh well...I was starting to feel more comfortable in Dubbo due to my friendships with Sa, Pat and, not to mention Bob, who kept Pat and I entertained at work with all his stories!

Despite this, I was hanging out for the pubs to open again so I could enjoy a nice counter meal and a few quiet beers in the relaxed atmosphere of what I was sure the many pubs in Dubbo offered. As I had discovered during drinking sessions in pubs all over the world, if you want to find out more about a new place, just spend an evening at one of the pubs chatting to the locals. Most of them had lived in the area their whole life, especially in small towns, so usually they had plenty of details to share to a newcomer over a few beers. I discovered the Loch Ness Monster was only a myth while chatting to a local at a pub in Edinburgh back in 2009. Fancy that hey. Could have fooled me! So, I have found there are certainly benefits from chatting to locals in pubs wherever I travel. I couldn't wait to also do it here in Dubbo – I just had to wait a little longer as the pandemic was still creating havoc and disrupting freedom, carving a void in your life. I was certainly going to appreciate all those things I did take for granted once we got the freedom to do them again. I just wished the pandemic would hurry up and piss off! I'm sure many people felt the same way.

Thirty-Four

Phoenix Rising from the Ashes

I started using the free time in a positive manner by going for long walks and just thinking about life. One chilly morning, I walked into town and down the main street. Seeing everything still closed due to the pandemic felt surreal. It felt like a ghost town and humanity had ceased to exist. It kind of reminded me of the American side of Niagara Falls from my visit there six years earlier. For a moment I thought of Marcia and what happened that weekend at Niagara Falls, but by this point in my life I was getting better at not dwelling on things that made me sad, so it was only a brief thought. The question of "what if" will always remain though.

I found myself walking along the Macquarie River a lot during that time as it soothed my soul. While on those walks, I felt something start to stir deep within my soul, especially as I walked along the riverbank. A little spark seemed to ignite in me. Could this be my time? Could my story arise from the pandemic like a phoenix rising from the ashes? Why not? The groundwork had been done. I felt it was time to really go for it and reach for the stars, to finally fulfil the potential my story had. It made me think of another quote I had read 'To give light one must first endure burning.' The coming years would determine how much of an impact my story could have on the world and what legacy I would leave behind long after I've gone.

If people still remembered my life, years after my passing, I would like to think Dubbo and the Macquarie River would be known as a pivotal place and part of my story.

The main key was to finally get my first book *One Eye. One Ear. No worries. A Story of Resilience* published. By now, Fleur only had one more section of editing to email through, so it was only a matter of time now. Then, just like that, fate seemed to answer my calling as I returned from my walk one evening to find she had emailed the final section through to me. You beauty! Being in Dubbo during a pandemic wasn't the ideal platform to publish a book, but I already knew what I was planning to do once I returned home, whenever that might be.

I was in a unique position with my boss letting me make the call on when I wanted to go home, but I was willing to stick it out as long as I could, at least until everything started to open again so I could experience the real Dubbo. I wanted to see this eerie quiet place come back to life as I believe it could be a vibrant city at its peak and not the ghost town I was becoming accustomed to.

When I wasn't at work, the only life in the town seemed to be the magic coming off the still water of the Macquarie River urging me to follow my calling, and it certainly had my attention. It would often be drizzling as I walked which would heighten my senses. I was certainly doing a lot of soul searching during my time in Dubbo as we headed into the cold winter months.

Finally, the premier of NSW announced sometime in late May, that places of entertainment such as pubs would gradually start to reopen again that weekend. Strict rules were in place though as only 10 patrons were allowed at any one time. You also had to be seated and could only stay for an hour. That didn't deter me as the thought of sitting down to enjoy a counter meal and a few beers in the relaxed atmosphere of a pub again sounded very enticing.

I had done my homework and found out the Westside Hotel was just around the corner from my accommodation. Perfect. I raced over and booked myself a table for 12 o'clock that Saturday. I woke early that morning feeling eager and a little excited. At the designated time I wandered over to the Westside, ordered a meal and beer and sat down at a table. I couldn't believe I was back in a pub setting! I noticed other patrons enjoying it as well, so I guess we were all in the same boat. The food was delicious, and I really savoured that beer. I only had one hour so to me it was just like Happy Hour. Bliss!

The following day I met up with Sa in the same park we caught up the first time. We were really enjoying each other's company as we got to know more about one another. We laughed as we sipped our beer, and I wondered if we would ever see each other again once we had left Dubbo. Either way, I was enjoying the moments we spent together. I found talking about my feelings came easily while I was with Sa, but I seem to do that naturally anyway. It was another magical day on what was an enjoyable weekend.

At work my friendship with Pat was coming along nicely. He was a family man and didn't drink, but we seemed to click. One day at work he asked what I was up to that evening as he was in the process of selling his house and building a new one and wanted to show me the new one that was being built. I was keen, as any human interaction outside of work hours had been scarce since the pandemic began. My catch ups with Sa were the only exception since I arrived in Dubbo. So, after work Pat picked me up from the front of my accommodation and drove to a new estate area just out of town. It was nice seeing another part of Dubbo. Making friends wherever I go has always been beneficial in making the most of a new experience. We also went out for dinner a few times and it was nice to experience Dubbo starting to come back to life as more rules were relaxed.

One Saturday morning I caught a taxi to Macquarie Street to start a pub crawl – a way to really experience all that Dubbo had to offer. At the first pub there was a guy playing bagpipes in the beer garden which took me back to my memories of travelling through Scotland. Listening to the sound of the pipes echoing through the chilly Dubbo wind took me back to when I was on the Royal Mile. Even though I wasn't overseas, in a kind of way it felt like I was travelling again. What a day this was already shaping up to be and it was only the first pub. It was in fact a great day as I checked out a few pubs along Macquarie Street, chatted to some locals, and even better, I arrived back at my hotel at a reasonable time.

It was around this time I received a call from my old friend Jono to ask if I would like the honour of being a groomsman for his wedding in Darwin the following year. I was overjoyed and immediately said yes. If I remember correctly, I also did a little dance in my room seeing as I had a few beers under my belt. Lol. Friendships have always been special to me. I've been meaning to make the trip up to visit Jono since he first moved to Darwin, and what better reason than to celebrate his wedding! The decision was made. I would be visiting the Top End as part of my travel plans the following year.

On a bit of a sad note, Sa's time in Dubbo was coming to an end, as she was planning on spending a few days in Sydney before heading home to France. One evening before she left, we went out for dinner to enjoy one last catch up together in Dubbo. Sa took me to a nice restaurant she often frequented. The evening had a feeling of finality as we were about to part ways, and I wondered if we would see one another again on our travels. I was confident we would meet again one day, seeing as catching up with friends around the world seems to be a regular occurrence in my life. I could see myself visiting France again. I was going to miss her company while here in Dubbo and I believe she felt the same way. Whatever happened next, I was happy that life or fate brought us together to share some special moments.

It felt like we were chatting for hours as it was turning into the night we didn't want to end. Finally, it came time to part ways, and I hoped Sa didn't detect the tears that fell from my eye onto her shoulder as I gave her a goodbye hug. Oh, the life of a traveller, forever saying "See you later" to people. The memories you share along the way always remain though. As I always say, "It's the people you meet and memories you create along the way that helps make the journey worthwhile." She also sent me a heartfelt voice message a few days later while she was in Sydney and about to head home to France. It really warmed my heart listening to it, especially when she said, "You have such an aura and energy that really shines from within. Thank you for your kindness and friendship. I was honoured to meet you in Dubbo as you are a beautiful soul and human." Thank you Sa for your heartwarming message before you left Australia.

Thirty-Five

Like a Man in Motion

With a long weekend coming up and seeing as the NSW premier had recently eased restrictions on travelling between regions, I figured it would be nice to get out of Dubbo for a weekend to check out a different part of NSW and maybe catch up with a friend while I'm at it. John Wong was another friend who I grew up with in Harvey who immediately came to mind. For anyone who has read my first book *One Eye. One Ear. No Worries*, you may recall a story I mentioned about John and me. He was back in Harvey from a stint in the army visiting family and we caught up for a few beers. Well, we ended up getting way too drunk on beer and Stones (whiskey) didn't we? Haha. We both ended up in a fair state that day much to the bemusement of John's mum once he had arrived back at her place after our drinking session. We both finally recovered from our escapades that day and stayed in touch over the years.

John (Wongy) had recently married, started a family and he and his partner had two young boys and were settled in Canberra these days. Catching up with Wongy and experiencing Canberra for the first time sounded like a wonderful way to spend a long weekend. I got in touch with Wongy and he was keen and excited to hear I was planning on heading to Canberra to see him. He even said he had a spare room for me to stay so I wouldn't have to book accommodation.

It was all set. I was heading to chilly Canberra. Just one problem. How am I going to get there? I could use the hire car, but that was to be used for work purposes only. Should I take the risk and use the hire car for a quick trip down to Canberra to catch up with Wongy? You betcha! I just won't claim travel allowance or petrol for that trip and with any luck my boss won't find out! And if he did, I'm sure he would be sweet about it as we got on so well. Plus, I had been restricted in my movements while in Dubbo up until that point, so I felt I was due a little freedom. A weekend away in Canberra was just what the doctor ordered!

It was roughly a five-hour drive, so I packed the hire car on Friday night and early on Saturday morning I left Dubbo destined for Canberra. Wongy was expecting me, and I couldn't wait to catch up with him again as it had been a while since we'd last seen each other. The scenery in NSW was magnificent as I glanced at some mountain ranges in the distance and wondered if they were the famous Blue Mountains. I felt so free driving along the highways of NSW after being restricted for a few months due to the pandemic. What a glorious June day it was.

I passed through some pretty towns which reminded me of growing up in Myalup and Harvey. Every town has a history and a story, and I've passed through many on my travels. Most also seem to have a servo and pub on the main street. Maybe some iconic feature that catches the eye of most travellers passing through. There's just something about small towns that really captures my imagination. Probably because of my own background. I stopped for a coffee at a café in one of the towns. It felt surreal enjoying a coffee in a town in rural NSW while a few months earlier I was stuck in lockdown in Katanning. We certainly took our freedom for granted. The world was changing and as a collective we had to learn to live with it. OK. My thoughts were starting to get away from me again. Time to hit the road and leave another random town behind. Onwards to the bright lights of Canberra.

As I got closer to Australia's largest inland city, I felt the temperature drop and the scenery become more mountainous as I approached the Australian Alps. Seeing as it was winter, I wondered if I would once again experience the beauty of snow. I finally arrived at a subdivision and pulled up at the address Wongy had sent me. I found myself out the front of a two-storey house at the end of a cul-de-sac and thought, "Wow, my old friend has done alright for himself." Wongy came out and greeted me warmly in the chilly weather and took me inside to introduce me to his partner Lauren and their two young sons. Before long, we were out on his back patio enjoying a beer and admiring the view. Wongy's house backed onto mountain ranges that overlooked a massive gully. It was an amazing sight as I took it all in. I was sure I could see snow on the tips of the mountains, or maybe it was just the foam from my stubby as the beers were going down well! Wongy then took me to a local pub for dinner and a few more beers. No beer and Stones this time! Haha. I was enjoying being in the company of my old friend as we shared plenty of stories and laughs. We ended the night huddled around a makeshift bonfire in his massive garage.

In the morning Wongy took me into the city to show me some of the sites. Unlike the other major cities in Australia, I noticed there weren't many, if any, skyscrapers in Canberra. As an example, it was in total contrast to the Gold Coast. While driving through the CBD I wondered if everyone I saw worked in the public sector as I currently did at that time in my life – we were in Canberra after all. Even though a lot of the attractions were closed due to Coronavirus and it being a long weekend we still visited some of the major sites such as the Australian War Memorial Museum at Old Parliament House, the National Science and Technology Centre and, of course, the new Parliament House which opened in our Bicentennial year of 1988.

We then went for lunch on the shores of Lake Burley Griffin. It was impressive seeing a jet of water shooting up in the centre of the lake. I was also impressed to hear it was an artificial lake. I was certainly getting the grand tour as Wongy then took me to the spot where he and Lauren were married. After that we headed up to Mount Ainslie Lookout to admire and appreciate views of the city. It was spectacular seeing the layout of the city from above. Wongy then gave me a wink to suggest it was time to go grab a beer somewhere. I certainly didn't need to be asked twice. Lol. We found a sports bar where we enjoyed a quiet beer on the way back to his house.

Once back at the house we enjoyed a few more. Lauren is also impressive at making cocktails, so she made a few for me to sample which I happily did. I felt like a connoisseur trying all these delicious cocktails that were being put in front of me. I guess it would have been a bit rude of me not to. Haha. It was another enjoyable evening with my friend and his family to finish my time in Canberra.

In the morning, Wongy cooked me a hearty breakfast, then after the usual goodbye to another friend which I had become all too accustomed to, I decided to get on the road early for the long drive back to Dubbo. While in Canberra I told Wongy where I was staying, and he must have looked it up as not long after I arrived back at my accommodation Wongy had sent me a gift. It was a book he figured I would like to have a look at as I do enjoy reading. It was his way of thanking me for visiting him in Canberra – and such a thoughtful gesture. Thanks, champ.

I had now been in Dubbo for roughly eight weeks, and I started to think of a suitable time to finally head home. Things were continuing to open, and I wanted to check out the zoo and the Old Dubbo Gaol while I was there. Sa had left and I could feel the pull of home growing stronger. I checked out the Old Dubbo Gaol first before I planned to spend a day out at the zoo. The main entrance was located off Macquarie Street. You wouldn't expect to find such a bleak and eerie place on such a lively street. Checking out the dark cells and seeing the re-erected gallows in the yard where convicts were hanged was a sobering experience. So many untold stories here. I felt a shudder as a cold chill rose up around me even though it was a relatively warm and sunny winter's day. I then went for a walk along the watchtower which offered great views of the town on one side while on the other you could look directly down into the gaol. Along with pubs, I believe two other places where you can learn about the history of a new place are museums and old historic gaols.

During my last few weeks in Dubbo, I went out for dinner with Pat again and I decided to spend the Saturday having one last pub crawl along Macquarie Street. I started at the Old Bank Bar around midday and over the course of the evening I also frequented the Establishment Bar among others before finishing up around the corner at the Pastoral Hotel. It was a jolly day with plenty of happy cheer. I had a feeling the publicans and barmaids were going to miss me when I left. I spoke to my boss and planned to do one more week at the Dubbo Meatworks before heading home. He seemed happy with that as I had already done a reasonably long stint over there. He asked if I wanted to fly out of Dubbo or would I rather drive the hire car down to Sydney and drop it off at the airport there? The thought of navigating the Sydney traffic sounded daunting, but on the other hand I would get the chance for a nice scenic drive through the Blue Mountains. That sounded enticing and helped sway my decision. I was willing to face the Sydney traffic for the chance to experience the Blue Mountains at my own leisurely pace. Bring it on!

Now that my travels home was all set, I decided to make the most of my last week while visiting the renowned Dubbo Zoo on my day off. I'm not usually one for visiting zoos on my travels, but I was fascinated by the prospect of seeing the lions and other animals from the wild up close. Even though the zoo was large, all the enclosures were within walking distance so it would give me a chance to do a bit of soul searching while walking along checking out the animals and maybe work up a thirst. I was spot-on with all three. It was an enjoyable experience and great finish to my time in Dubbo.

While having a few beers and listening to music during the weekends in Dubbo, I found myself listening to the song "St Elmo's Fire (Man in Motion)" by John Parr quite often. I found that song to be uplifting and the lyrics were helping to stir up this feeling inside of me, the feeling that maybe this was my time. I knew what I had to do once I arrived back home. I certainly felt like a man in motion and that the world was ready to hear my story. I just had to survive the traffic in Sydney first! I had spent 10 weeks in Dubbo, arriving during the height of the pandemic, and I felt I had used this experience to really grow as a person. Even though it was challenging at times, I had stuck it out and gained some wisdom which I would take with me into the future by opting to travel during a pandemic.

My last day at the Dubbo Meatworks was filled with the usual goodbyes and I had the hire car packed on Friday night ready for my journey to

Sydney on the Saturday. I planned to hit the road early in the morning and before I left I went for one last walk through the park to the banks of the Macquarie, and while taking it all in, I wondered if I would be back one day. If I ever did visit again, I was sure the Macquarie River will be there waiting for me. Then I was off, bound once again for the harbour city. I wondered how people used to navigate before the days of GPS and the good old street directory came to mind. It was a five-hour drive with the luxury of seeing the scenic Blue Mountains along the way.

The first half of the drive was relatively boring but as I passed through the town of Lithgow beautiful scenery started to form in front of me. As I started to gain altitude while driving into the mountains, I noticed the road included a lot of sharp twists and turns which kept me alert. I passed through plenty of dense forests and spotted a few signs leading to breathtaking waterfalls while craning my neck to catch a glimpse of the falls as I drove.

Whenever I passed a clearing in the dense forest I would quickly look out over the vast landscape trying to catch a glance of the Three Sisters. Oops. I almost went off the road. I had to keep my wits about me, and this was meant to be the easy part of the journey! I still had the busy city traffic to contend with yet! Gulp... I stopped at a gift shop to get a better view of the landscape as it was situated in a clearing overlooking a massive gully. Even a gift shop can be used as a low lookout, and I certainly took advantage of it. I felt inspired standing in the mist of the Blue Mountains, energised enough to handle the upcoming Sydney traffic. It was impressive!

After taking it all in I took a deep breath and got back in the car as I wasn't sure what I was heading into. I noticed the roads starting to get busier as I drove into the outer suburbs. Gulp...here goes! Can't turn back now as I had to get the hire car to Sydney Airport, hopefully with very little or no damage. I popped in for a visit with Louisa and Adrian for an hour or so while I was passing through. As always, they were happy to see me, and it was great catching up with them to break up the journey. Before leaving Louisa's, I had a good look over the car to check for any damage, as any further damage from then would be on me! As I got closer to the city,

I felt the traffic becoming more congested. My heart was racing as I was beginning to rue my decision to drive the hire car the whole way to Sydney Airport. Luckily it was insured, but I didn't need the stress of having to tell my boss I had an accident, and the hire car was at the wreckers. But "I'm all good and I'll be right to board the plane tomorrow" I told myself. No, try not to think of that outcome. I'm going to get the car to the airport in good condition.

Suddenly the traffic started speeding up so, in turn, I also put my foot down on the pedal a little to gain speed. Now it was starting to feel real. I was in-sync with the traffic as we approached the Sydney Harbour Tunnel. The intensity level went up a notch as we all entered the tunnel. Wow, this was intense! I kept glancing at the speedometer then back to the road. I had to keep my wits about me while also making sure I kept to the speed limit. As we exited the tunnel I could see Sydney Harbour bridge behind me in the distance through the rearview mirror. I suddenly had a sense of nostalgia as I thought back to all the memories I had made here. My thoughts started to wander. Honk!!! Oh ****, got to keep my eye on the road. Stay focused, now is not the time for reminiscing. I went to change lanes and heard another honk, so I decided to stay put in the lane I was in.

The traffic in Sydney was beyond hectic and I was right amongst it. Surely the airport can't be too far away now. Suddenly the signs to the terminals came into view as I started to breathe a sigh of relief. Honk!!! Oh ****. Can't relax just yet. I drove into the airport and figured the worst was over as all I had to do now was to find the Avis car rental bay and drop the car off. Unfortunately, it was like finding a needle in a haystack as I did at least 20 laps of the airport before I finally found it deep in the bowels of the undercover parking area. That was a mission. A guy walked out from inside a small glass room, and I gently threw the keys to him as he would take care of it from here. No damage. Thank God.

I was staying in the same hotel as when I first came over, so I found it quite easily. While relaxing in my room I received a reply to a message I sent to Tonia earlier to let me know she already had plans so couldn't catch up this time. Totally understandable as it was short notice, and I was only passing through Sydney this time on my way home. I was sure we would get a chance to catch up again when I visited Sydney in the future. Plus, I had had enough excitement for one day as I could still hear the honks of the car horns from the hectic Sydney traffic ringing in my ear. Lucky I only had one. Lol.

Thirty-Six

The Power of a Friendship Bracelet

While walking to the airport in the crisp morning air I noticed there was a bit more activity happening around me from when I was last there, ten weeks earlier. I boarded the plane as my thoughts started to focus on home and what was to come. I had prophesized it while I was in Dubbo so it was now time to put it into action to see how far my story could go. I was boosted! Just had to get back into WA first.

Upon landing I confidently walked up to the customs officials and showed them the letter stating I was an essential worker returning home from employment duties over east. Like most people in authority seem to do, he kept me hanging as a man with a stern look on his face went over the contents of the letter. I took a gulp as my confidence slowly melted away. I wondered if he was a slow reader, or he just enjoyed keeping me in the lurch. Power does funny things to people as the stern expression never left his face. His demeanour made me feel like I was returning to the state as a parolee. Finally, he spoke. Man, that felt like an eternity! I was so happy to hear I didn't have to go into hotel quarantine, which was lucky as the only book I had in my luggage was the gift from Wongy. But seeing as WA had pretty much cut itself off from the rest of the world to become its own fortress, I did have to quarantine at a nominated address, so I gave him my parents' address.

Mum and Dad picked me up from the airport and I couldn't wait to get in the car to take my mask off for a while. Bliss. At this stage my brother Kelvin had his own place next door to Mum and Dad so I spent the following two weeks between the two houses. Kelvin's place had a veranda which offered great views of the lake in the distance so naturally I found it a suitable place to read and write. It was easy to be inspired while looking out at the stillness of the lake. I read Paul Carter's *Don't tell mum I work on the Rigs* as I found his humour hilarious and could relate to his writing and experiences. Plenty of funny stories that kept me entertained while in quarantine. Kelvin popped his head out a few times to see what I was laughing at. Kelvin and I have always been close, and we had some good chats during that time. As a younger brother I was proud of where he was at in life. He had a stint with his own segment on the local radio and he played a part in a movie that recently premiered in Perth called *Anticipation*. If my memory serves me well I also started writing this second book while in quarantine, so I found it to be a useful experience.

Fleur had finished editing the first book, but I couldn't do much while I was in Dubbo, and quarantine was the only obstacle in my way now. The dream of having my book published was now within reach. Naturally, once I was released from quarantine I met up with Fleur in Bunbury at a café on the waterfront. I now find myself inspired around water. Fleur gave me a printout of the word document she had created from my handwritten manuscript. I could feel my book starting to come to life. It felt unreal as I glanced out over the water. I figured the handwritten manuscript may be worth something one day – or it may not, but it was a nice thought. While sitting there with Fleur that on the waterfront I thought about how the pandemic had come along to keep people apart and yet here we were coming together to accomplish something special. Our lives may have been disrupted but we were coming out the other side and doing our best to move forward.

After seeing Fleur, I headed over to the Prince to catch up with my friend Katie while she was on her lunch break. While on the way over I thought about our friendship which went way back. Katie was a few years younger than me and had also grown up in Harvey. Like many other friendships that have stood the test of time, ours started in that town as we played on the same mixed netball team called The Delinquents. I had a bit of a teenage crush on Katie so one day I bought her a friendship bracelet as a gift. I was a little shy at that time in my life, so nothing eventuated between us beyond the friendship, and like most kids who grew up in small towns, we found our own paths in life.

But never underestimate the power of a friendship bracelet as it must have worked its magic. No matter how long it had been since we last saw or spoke to one another, Katie always seemed to sense whenever I was feeling low and needed to hear from a friend, so she would reach out, wherever in the world I might be. Sweden comes to mind. Reading her messages of support never failed to lift my spirits and gave me the extra strength I needed to face whatever darkness I was going through at that time in my life. They say you can go ages without hearing from certain friends, but whenever you need a friend, they always seem to pop up and that is Katie. She speaks from the heart, so she was delighted to include an intro for this book.

With the editing of the book now completed we enjoyed a few drinks at the Prince to celebrate. I'm pretty sure Katie had an extended lunch break that day. Haha. Even though she was busy with her own life, her supportive nature comes to the fore to help whenever she can. Legend in my book!

Now I just needed to find a publisher. Where do I start? I looked up a local publisher and a few days later I pulled up in their driveway bursting with anticipation. A guy came out, and without getting out of the car as some Covid restrictions were still in place, I handed him the manuscript to see if he was interested in publishing it. He took a quick glance through it then handed it back without showing much interest. He told me to email it online and they will let me know. Turning up in person didn't get me the result I expected so I had a lot to learn about the publishing industry. "What a fool," I thought as I drove away. He didn't even realise the potential of the story he briefly had in his hands. I tried a few different publishers with pretty much the same result. All these publishers are fools I thought.

Around that time, Nina, who was a good friend of Kelvin's, sent me the link to a self-publishing group she knew based in Nannup called

Pickawoowoo. A great idea came to me. Seeing as it was my story, instead of giving it to someone else, why not keep control of it all as the writer and publisher. I believed it had the potential of being a great read. Why not see how far I could take it on my own? I looked up at the sky and decided that was the limit. So, I phoned Pickawoowoo and spoke to Julie-Ann who was more than happy for me to self-publish my book. So that is how my first book *One Eye. One Ear. No worries* came about. As they say, the rest is history. So, I sent Pickawoowoo the Manuscript and now it became a waiting game.

Thirty-Seven

THE STARS ALIGN

Coming out of winter that year of 2020 I was based back in Bunbury for employment when one day my boss phoned to see if I was interested in filling in down at Cowaramup, either for a few weeks or for the duration of summer. My accommodation would be in Margaret River during the week, and I could spend the weekends back home. How could I say no to that? I've been based down that way for work before, so I've had a taste of what Margaret River has to offer.

I settled into that lifestyle easily. I became a hippie, grew my hair long and surfed the latest waves on my long board like a pro surfer. Haha. Only joking, but I could see how that kind of lifestyle could really influence people as we are often the product of our environment. I also found Margaret River to have a very creative vibe as it seemed to attract not only surfers and sharks, but also artists, writers, musicians and maybe even candlestick makers. All walks of life seemed to gravitate to that part of the world. No wonder it is known all over the world as a popular destination. It is also well known for its breweries and wineries throughout the region. It is a place to really inspire creativity. With my book on the verge of being published, maybe I had come to the right place.

After work I would often spend my afternoons going for walks through the forest while looking up at the karri trees. I discovered some nice paths which led to flowing rivers. I found I was moving into a more creative phase of my life during my time in Margaret River. As a would-be author, I had come to the right place. One day after work I went for a drive to check out Prevelly Beach. It was a bleak and overcast spring day, and as I looked out to the horizon I noticed what looked to be a storm brewing in the distance. It didn't seem to faze the local surfers though as they seemed at ease navigating the choppy waters. I thought they were either brave or crazy being out there in that weather as I was more than happy to watch them from the safety of the carpark. I often wondered if the people of Margaret River knew they had a would-be author in their midst. It was just a matter of waiting now.

Then, just before Christmas, the big day finally arrived as Julie-Ann sent me the first-ever published copy of my book. I couldn't describe the feeling of finally holding the published copy in my hands. To say I was over the moon is an understatement. The cover looked good too, and I knew it would draw people in. Following the pandemic in 2020, the following year was looming as a pretty big one with book launches and author talks to come. I was ecstatic! And, to think I could have easily gone down a different path!

During the winter of 2015 I was going through a bit of a bleak time in my life and a good mate I was catching up with quite a bit around that time was also going through a bit. That was during the time I was living with Frog in the house next to the shop and my mate would often come down from Perth over the weekends. One day we were watching a documentary on the drug meth and how it was becoming a scourge to society. I said to my mate, "I wonder what the big attraction must be as so many people seem to be getting hooked on it?" Oh well, I guess there was only one way to find out. What were we thinking? As if I hadn't been reckless enough during the party years of my youth. I just had to experience everything, didn't I?

One thing led to another and later that evening we finally got our hands on enough meth to last the weekend. My friend had made us a makeshift pipe to smoke it through. He also had his bourbons, and I had my beers, so we were all set! Time to get the party started as I took a toke from the pipe. Wow!!! It pretty much hit me straight away as a feeling of euphoria washed over me. My friend and I were chatting and suddenly whatever we were both going through didn't seem that bad anymore. Everything was great with the world.

That night another friend phoned to see what we were up to. He wanted to join us but seeing as he was going through some dramas in his relationship he decided he better stay with his missus to hopefully work things out. An hour or so later there was a knock at the door. It was our friend, and he was alone. He sat down on the couch and took a big toke on the pipe. It was now a party of three! A few days later he was still sitting in that exact same spot! He suddenly remembered it was Sunday and he had promised to cook a roast turkey for his in-laws who were coming around for dinner that night. He got up and left. Suffice to say that relationship didn't survive. I never did ask my friend how dinner with his missus and the in-laws went. To be honest, it's probably better that I don't know – it can't have been a good scene.

The following weekend my friend and I discussed and analysed the experience. We both agreed we had danced with the devil and came out the other side with the wisdom to say we won't ever be doing that again! Thankfully, we never have.

While holding my book and thinking back to that bleak winter of 2015 it was scary to think I was at a crossroads in my life and could have easily gone down a different path. My friend and I had a glimpse into the abyss and quickly pulled back before it could consume us. My book may have never come to fruition if the meth had taken a hold of me. John Lennon from The Beatles famously had a lost weekend which lasted from mid-1973 to early 1975. Luckily for me and my two friends, our lost weekend of 2015 only lasted a few days!

Oh wait, where was I? Ah yes, the end of 2020 and I was now an author. Just not a well-known one so it was time to learn on the go how to promote and market myself. Being based in a place like Margaret River at that point in my life was always going to be beneficial. I knew Fiona from my Zoom meetings with Ben which I wrote about earlier in this book. She lived in Margaret River with her husband Christo, so the stars seemed to be lining up for me. Fiona is very ambitious and such a lovely person from what I gathered on our Zoom sessions. So, I reached out to her to let her know I was currently in town and before I knew it we were meeting up for dinner at a local brewery where I had the pleasure of also meeting Christo.

I was right with my intuition as they were both great people. Very easy-going and engaging. Fiona also seemed to have so many contacts; I was in elite company. So, it came as no surprise when she mentioned she was good friends with the old couple who ran the local bookstore on the main street in town and they may be interested in helping me out as a new author. "I will drink to that," I said as I took a swig of my beer. Almost every other patron in the brewery that evening knew Fiona and Christo, so it seems I have a bit of a knack of finding myself in the right circles. In a few years they would have the grand opening of their own winery, but I will save that for my next book. I took a photo with Fiona and Christo holding a copy of my book, so maybe I did have a bit of marketing sense about me already! All up, it was a great evening and the start of another good friendship.

Through Fiona's friendship I got to meet Keith and Pauline, and they were more than happy to help a new author out by hosting a book launch at their store. Even better, they would help promote it. So, my first-ever book launch was to be held in Margaret River on the 1st of April 2021. This was just the start of what was to come, as one day in early March, Studio 10 which is based in Sydney reached out to see if I would be interested in going on their programme to share my story and promote my book. I couldn't believe it! I pinched myself a few times! Ouch!!! I certainly wasn't dreaming. This was really happening! So, I booked the day off work and headed up to the Channel 10 Studios in Perth to conduct the interview with the host from Sydney. While the cameramen helped me adjust the headset and microphone it started to dawn on me my story was reaching a whole new level of awareness. While looking out the window from one of the higher floors I could see in the distance the spot where Princess Margaret Hospital used to be, and it brought back so many memories from my childhood as I took another trip down memory lane. It was as if my life had now gone full circle. I felt emotional as I wiped a tear away from my eye. Suddenly the bright lights came on and it was showtime!

I was in my element as I told stories of all the ears and eyes I lost during my adventurous childhood as well as using my glass eye as a marble in schoolyard games. I also promoted my book every chance I got. The hosts loved it, and I couldn't be happier with how it all went. Just before I went on, I received a text from my good mate Calvin, so I gave him a shout out on air along with my two brothers.

Not long after my segment on Studio 10, I got in touch with Tom who was happy to do a follow up on my story and the recent book release. We met up once again on the shores of Koombana Bay in Bunbury. I was starting to get the hang of these television interviews as it all now seemed to flow naturally. As part of the self-publishing service people could buy my book from any of the major online platforms, so my friends and others who had heard of my story were already purchasing my book online. The promotional side of things seemed to be taking care of itself. For all the negatives surrounding it, I also found Facebook to be a useful promotional tool. In fact, I was using whatever tool I could to my advantage when it came to promoting the book. I even tried photography with startling results! What I had envisioned while walking along the Macquarie River back in Dubbo was starting to manifest.

Then the big one happened! As if it was part of my destiny, I walked into the office of my old school, Harvey Primary, holding a copy of my book and asked if I could talk to the principal. We sat down in his office for a chat, and he was delighted to hear he not only had a former pupil of the school in his midst, but also an author! A book launch at my old school would be such a special moment for me and he agreed so he planned the launch to take place on the 24th of May 2021.

So now it was all set as I had a book launch planned for Margaret River and one for Harvey. But I had Jono's buck's party to get through and hopefully survive first! I had heard a lot about Big J from Jono over the years. He was going to be the best man and someone I would soon have the pleasure of meeting. Let's hope the legend lived up to the hype! I would soon find out. Big J planned the buck's party and as expected, he pulled out all the stops by planning a four-day bender in Fremantle for a weekend in late March.

It wasn't even a long weekend! It was now! Lol. Even though Jono and I had remained friends, life had taken us on different paths since our travels through Europe and I was really looking forward to seeing him again after so long. I just hoped my liver was ready! Surely it wasn't going to be Europe all over again as we were starting to get a bit old for that! Lol. But from what I had heard about Big J, I certainly had my doubts of it being a tame weekend. It was going to be epic and loose!

I decided to skip the Thursday night celebrations and head up on the Friday morning to meet up with Jono and everyone else at the share house Big J had booked for us in Freo. Looking back now, it was probably a wise move. On the evening before I headed up to Freo I met up with Coralee in Harvey as she wanted to receive a signed copy of my book. Wonderful Coralee, always so supportive. She also assured me she would be attending my upcoming book launch at our old school Harvey Primary.

The following morning, I drove up to Freo to meet Jono and the others at the share house. Once I arrived, I parked my car out of the way as I knew I wouldn't be needing it for a few days. As expected, it was great seeing Jono again and to be introduced to the other guys. Introductions had barely finished when we found ourselves at the Little Creatures Brewery sampling the local ales. It was on!

I found Big J to be a larger-than-life character; he was certainly living up to the hype. He reminded me of my buddy Shaban back in Melbourne. I had a feeling Big J felt the same about me as we got to know one another that first day. According to the others, Jono's brother in-law, Lumbo, could sometimes get a bit much after a few drinks. I found him friendly enough, though the stories he was telling did seem to get more outrageous the more he drank! As a joke, Jono and his brother Tony did ask the barmaid if she would spike his drink to calm him down but to no avail! Lol. We then headed to a popular bar in Freo before finishing the night back at the share house. Phew!!! I survived day one.

The following morning, we met up with more of the crew to do a boat cruise on the Swan River. We all received stubby holders with our names on them. So I was sure I wouldn't lose mine! It was a great day on the water as the beers flowed and the happy cheer grew louder. We all managed to get our second wind as we kicked on at another pub in Freo that night. I noticed everyone was still dry, so no one had fallen overboard that I knew of. Happy cheer was certainly echoing throughout Freo that night. Jono had finally brought me and Big J together as the revelries continued well into the night. Phew!!! It was a close call, but I survived day two.

Day three was a struggle as the few of us who were left headed to another pub for a Sunday sesh. Lumbo had a sip of his beer, then excused himself to go to the toilet. We never saw him again that day. The casualty list was growing. The five or so of us left continued to push through. Drink up boys! Boost! The last hurrah. Phew!!! It was a struggle, but we stayed the course. I never thought drinking beer could feel like a marathon, but here we were. We kept a lid on the happy cheer as we crawled to a few different pubs in Freo that evening. Phew!!! I survived day three. In the morning, the boys started chatting about day four as I politely made my excuses and left for home. I couldn't do another day. Sorry fellas. Lol. If the buck's celebration was anything to go by, the wedding up in Darwin in July was going to be epic! A few weeks in the Top End. What could go wrong?

Thirty-Eight

The World is Your Oyster

On the evening of the 1st of April, I headed down to Margaret River with Mum and Nanna for my first-ever book launch. The local radio phoned me, and I gave an interview while on the way down. Keith, Pauline, Fiona and Christo were already there and had done a great job setting up the bookstore for the launch. Fiona was a blessing as she was such a bubbly burst of positive energy. None of this would have been possible without her. A total of 13 people ended up attending my book launch that night which I saw as a success because I wasn't from Margaret River, and you must start somewhere. It could only get bigger. All 13 people purchased a book, as I discovered the joy and fulfilment of book signing! I'm sure they all went away inspired that night. I was excited by what was to come.

The lead up to my next book launch at Harvey Primary School was buzzing to say the least. I had to pinch myself... Ouch! No, I wasn't dreaming. The town seemed to be getting behind it. I ordered 50 copies of my book for the night. The buzz was incredible. It was shaping up to be a night of celebration surrounded by family and friends as the anticipation continued to build. Finally, the big night arrived. Even though I received some well-wishes from friends who couldn't make it, I was anticipating a big turnout. Like the TED talk I did four years earlier, this was shaping up to be another big moment in my life. I was going back to my old school where it had begun all those years ago. Though the temptation may have been there, I had to remind myself not to use my glass eye as a marble this time! Lol.

I noticed that the principal, Mr Romeo, had done a wonderful job setting up the new staff room for my launch as I walked in. It was great to have him on board. I was starting to feel like a proper author as we arranged and set up the 50 copies of my book on a table. I had to quickly pinch myself again... Ouch! Once again, I found I wasn't dreaming. This was happening! People started turning up as I mingled. So many familiar faces who had been a part of my journey in some capacity. What a catch-up this was going to be! Before long, the room was packed! MLA Robyn Clark and her husband were also invited and came along.

Before long, Mr Romeo made a speech before handing it over to me. I had my slideshow of pics up behind me and from the moment I started speaking I felt relaxed as everyone in the audience was there to support me. During this speech I looked around at all the familiar faces in the crowd. My lovely family who has been there from the start, Normie, Leanne, Ken, Katie, Ash, Mark, Coralee, Jade, Jolly, Wardy, PJ's Mum Leigh, Anthony Chero, Paul Commisso, Belle and so many more. Boo Boo (Shawn) couldn't make it as he had work commitments up north, but his partner Carissa and two children were there on his behalf. His Mum and in-laws were also there. Good job bud. Adam and Nancy also couldn't make it. I noticed Katie coming in halfway through my speech. Good old Katie. Better late than never.

It was another emotional moment in my life, and I felt a tear leave my eye. I had shared so many good times and memories with these people over the years and this was another one. As soon as I finished I received a massive ovation which seemed to last forever. It was hard not to get caught up in the moment as my emotion started to get the better of me. Then it was time to mingle and sign some books! I felt I was in my element. I was chatting to someone when Coralee came up with a shriek of excitement and gave me a big hug, as did Katie. A local family whose son also had a facial disfigurement was there that night. I'm sure they took a lot away from hearing my speech. Honestly, the night couldn't have been more magical. More than 60 people attended, and I sold all 50 copies of my book! So that was where I was at this stage in my life. A first-time author with plenty of hometown support.

I believe I have grown and learned more about myself these last few years from where I was at the start of 2018 and the year I finished my first book. Due to circumstances that were out of my control, I couldn't experience much overseas travel during this period in my life. But on the other hand, I was fortunate enough to see a lot more of Australia and gain appreciation of what our own country has to offer. In saying that, having a hiatus from overseas travel, made me realise how much I missed it. I still hope to experience places such as Croatia, Slovenia, Greece, Norway and Finland among others. I've heard the sunsets in Greece and Croatia are spectacular! Maybe I'll get to see them one day. I also haven't given up hope of being allowed to visit Canada again at some stage and to see more of the US. Maybe some of my best travel experiences are still in front of me? As the saying goes, the world is your oyster.

During different stages in this follow-up book, I touched on my binge drinking and where I was with that. Even though I feel I'll always enjoy the social aspect of having a few beers with mates, it is something I will continue working on moving forward as I am making progress. I don't need to be the life of the party forever, though I do feel that little spark in me will never completely go out. I also hope to continue sharing my story to see how far it can go and how much of a difference it can make. Maybe this is my time to make an impact that could endure beyond the grave.

Like a Brave

You must use the light to find your way
because nothing golden can ever stay
Be the creator of your own story
and you will hopefully find a path that leads to glory.
Always keep fighting like a brave
and you will find that memories can live on even beyond the grave.

Editor's Note

Coralee Italiano was born and raised in Harvey.

A former journalist, turned educationalist, she is passionate about sharing stories and helping others achieve their dreams.

As a life-long friend of Joel, she was excited and honoured about the opportunity to collaborate with him on this project.

Coralee hopes that Joel's story of travelling and friendships around Australia inspires others to also be brave; take that leap and spread their wings.

www.ingramcontent.com/pod-product-compliance
Lightning Source LLC
Chambersburg PA
CBHW062035290426
44109CB00026B/2637